Doorway at Auchendoir

MEDIEVAL CHURCHES
OF SCOTLAND

Mike Salter

FOLLY PUBLICATIONS

ACKNOWLEDGMENTS

The plans and maps were all drawn by the author. The plans are based on surveys made during the author's many field trips in Scotland between 1977 and 2010. Charles Henderson of Auchtermuchty provided pictures of Auchendoir, Temple and the church of St Leonard at St Andrews, other pictures used in this book's predecessor (see below), plus occasional accommodation. Thanks are also due to John and Nancy Wright of Plean for help and accommodation. Kate Miles provided the pictures of Orphir, Abercorn, Duffus, Eynhallow, Grandtully, Pencaitland, Tullibardine and Uphall. All the other photos were either taken by the author or are from the author's collection, eg the old postcards of Biggar, Egilsay and Whitekirk. Thanks are also due to Max Barfield, Helen Thomas and Jenny Harper, who have all driven author across Scotland at some time, and to Janet and John Walton for help with accommodation on Shetland and the loan of a car there which was driven by Jean Cuddeford. Paul and Allan at Aspect Design also need to be thanked for help with the cover details and the layout design, and Paul Adkins for sorting out a computer crisis shortly before the book was completed.

AUTHOR'S NOTES

This book supersedes the author's previous work The Old Parish Churches of Scotland published in 1994. That book included buildings up to 1700 but this one uses the Scottish Reformation Parliament of 1560 as a cut-off point in deciding what to include, although there are, of course, a number marginal buildings such as the tower at Inverness which may or may not have already been under construction by that date. This book considerably updates and improves on the earlier title. The plans are now all on the single scale of 1:400, allowing useful comparisons with plans of similar buildings in England, Wales and Ireland which appear in the other volumes of this series.

Although cathedrals in Scotland and many of the monastic churches there also functioned as parish churches (and some still do to this day), these buildings are not included here since they are fully described and illustrated by the same author in the companion volume Medieval Abbeys and Cathedrals of Scotland.

Nearly all the buildings described in this book are readily accessible to the general public. Many of the churches are ruins that can be freely visited at any time, although any right of access through an estate to them may only be on foot. One or two buildings lie hidden away deep in estates close to the owners' houses (eg at Yester) so permission and directions should be sought before visiting. Roofed buildings may only be accessible at certain times, and visitors will have to pay fees to visit the churches or chapels at Lincluden, Rosslyn, Seton, and that of St Regulus at St Andrews.

ABOUT THE AUTHOR

Mike Salter is 57 and has been a professional writer and publisher since he went on the Government Enterprise Allowance Scheme for unemployed people in 1988. He is particularly interested in the planning and layout of medieval buildings and has a huge collection of plans of churches and castles he has measured during tours (mostly by bicycle, motorcycle or on foot) throughout all parts of the British Isles since 1968. Originally from Wolverhampton, Mike now lives in an old cottage beside the Malvern Hills. His other interests include walking, maps, railways, board games, all kinds of morris dancing, mumming, playing percussion instruments and calling folk dances.

Copyright 2011 by Mike Salter.   First published March 2011
Folly Publications, Folly Cottage, 151 West Malvern Rd, Malvern, Worcs, WR14 4AY
Printed by Aspect Design, 89 Newtown Rd, Malvern, Worces WR14 2PD

Last remains of the circular nave and apse at Orphir in Orkney

CONTENTS

Maps occur at the end of each other churches section

INTRODUCTION

Christianity first reached Scotland at the beginning of the 5th century when St Ninian set up a bishopric at Whithorn which lasted until the 8th century. Dalriada or Argyll was Christian by the early 6th century, and in 563 St Columba established a monastery on Iona. Missionaries from both Iona and Whithorn were sent out to convert other parts of Scotland, Dunblane for example having been a religious centre since c600. By the 9th century the Norsemen who controlled Orkney, Shetland and the Hebrides until the mid 13th century were mostly Christian and a diocese of Orkney (which included Shetland) was established c1050. The many places with names beginning with Kil- are thought to have had chapels either of wood or stone by the 8th century. The main religious centres of the Celtic church were run by secular priests known as Culdees (properly Celi Dei - Clients of God), who were allowed to marry and pass on hereditary offices.

The papacy gradually re-established its authority over the Celtic religious centres from the 8th century onwards but it was not until the 12th century that a proper Roman system of parish churches grouped together to form dioceses ruled by bishops was established in Scotland. The 12th and 13th centuries also saw the founding of many new houses of monks, regular canons and nuns belonging to one of the monastic orders approved by the Roman Church. In medieval Scotland the naves or western parts monastic churches and cathedrals often performed parochial functions but these generally larger buildings form the subject of a companion volume. This book, concerns itself with purely parochial churches, collegiate churches, and other chapels serving a variety of functions but mostly as chapels-of-ease to parish churches.

Footings of early chapel at St Blane's on Bute

Window of 12th century tower at Muthil

Kilmichael Chapel on Bute

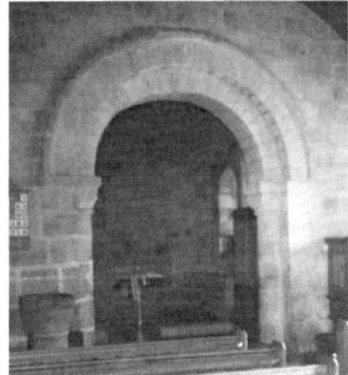

Chancel arch at Birnie

Malcolm III's spouse Margaret, a devout Saxon princess in exile from England's new Norman rulers, began the process of reorganising the Scottish church late in the 11th century and it continued under the successive reigns of their three sons Edgar, d1107, Alexander, d1124, and David, d1154. Some remote districts only gained their own parish churches in the later medieval period and the system has never been static. Small parishes were sometimes amalgamated. Larger or more populous parishes might be divided when a former chapel-of-ease finally attained full parochial status. Scottish churches were often wrecked during wars and occasionally were replaced by other buildings on new sites. By the later medieval period there were cathedrals at Aberdeen, Brechin, Dornoch, Dunblane, Dunkeld, Elgin, Fortrose, Glasgow, Kirkwall, Lismore, St Andrews and Whithorn and several hundred parish churches on the Scottish mainland. Orkney, Shetland and the inner and outer Hebrides had at least another 60 parish churches, these remote islands also having many small humble chapels of ease.

Rosyth Church

Although there are many crosses and carved stones remaining from the period before the 12th century reorganisation of the Scottish church, and some of the banks and walls surrounding churchyards may be of very great age, not much remains of early churches in Scotland. Some of the crosses may have marked outdoor places where people gathered for worship. Small early stone chapels remain beside Whithorn Cathedral and Iona Abbey. Many other small featureless chapels (many of them drystone structures now reduced to footings) in the Highlands and Islands could be of almost any date up to the 17th century. On the mainland some early churches may have been of wood, and standing stone structures earlier than David I's reign are few. Restenneth Priory has an early 12th century tower raised over a possible 8th century porch. The church of St Regulus at Andrews has a tall 11th century tower which served as a nave and a landmark for mariners. Footings of a similar tower-nave have been found under the abbey church at Dunfermline. At Abernethy and Brechin are 11th century round towers of the type still common in Ireland, but no early churches or chapels now remain at either of these places.

Church of St Regulus at St Andrews

The fine 12th century church at Dalmeny

Abbey churches and cathedrals were often cruciform structures with central towers and long naves divided by arcades of circular columns from side aisles but rural parish churches of the 12th century were much smaller and simpler. Including examples from the offshore islands of Iona, Islay, Lewis, Orkney and Shetland about fifty churches with considerable work in them of c1125-1200 still remain in Scotland. Some were single rectangular chambers with just a wooden screen dividing the nave for the congregation from the chancel containing the altar. Many rural medieval parish churches and chapels in Scotland retained this plain and simple form right up to the Reformation. Early churches of this type usually had small round-headed windows on either side near the altar at the east end, a window in the east wall, and a doorway near the west end of the south wall. By c1200 pairs of windows began to appear in the east wall.

Mostly scattered around the Firth of Forth and the Borders are over twenty 12th century churches with a shorter and narrower chancel at the east end of the nave or evidence that such existed. All have been much altered in subsequent periods. Examples are Aberdour, Duddingston, Gullane, Legerwood, Linton, Ratho, Smailholm and Stobo, whilst Birnie is an isolated specimen further north and Cruggleton is a much rebuilt example in Galloway. Lasswade and Uphall had in addition a tower west of the nave. Tyninghame, now mostly reduced to footings, and Dalmeny, the best preserved 12th century parish church in Scotland, had both a west tower and an apse beyond the chancel. A vaulted apse survives on its own at Bunkle and a larger example with its chancel at Leuchars, where both parts are covered externally by blind arcading. There is another apse at Borthwick and bases of others have been excavated at Aberdeen and Hirsel. In Norse-held Orkney there is a church with an east apse and a west porch or tower at Brough of Birsay. A second tiny apse at Orphir projects east from meagre remains of the only recorded medieval circular nave in Scotland, probaby inspired by a sucessful pilgrimage to Jerusalem. Another Norse-built vaulted apse survives at Thurso. It has a rectangular exterior like the apse of St Margaret's Chapel at Edinburgh Castle. Another 12th century Orkney church is Egilsay, where the square chancel is vaulted and there is a circular west tower like those found in East Anglia and Sussex.

Good square west towers of c1200 remain at Dunning, Kirkliston and Markinch. Slightly earlier towers at Dunblane Cathedral and Muthil may have been detached until churches were later built around them. Of 12th century parochial town churches on a larger scale there remain only the crossing arches and transepts at Aberdeen and the west wall of an aisled nave at Ayr. Rutherglen also once had a fully aisled 12th century nave five bays long. Airth had a north aisle with a three bay arcade by c1200 and St Vigeans gained one aisle in the 13th century and another in the 15th century. Longitudinal aisles flanking the full length of a nave were never common in Scotland. Only about two dozen of the ordinary parish churches ever had aisles of this type (which were common enough even in small rural churches in England), and nearly all of the Scottish examples were in market towns such as Lanark or Dalkeith or flourishing ports along the coasts of Fife and Lothian such as Crail, Dysart and North Berwick.

The tower at Markinch

In the early 13th century the pointed arch gradually replaced the round arch. Tall single light windows of this era are called lancets. New ideas only slowly worked their way out to remote areas, and the position is complicated by 12th and 13th century features re-appearing in the late medieval period (for instance the twin lancet window in the east wall at Alloway is probably 16th century). This can make accurate dating of buildings difficult, especially as there are few historical records of work done upon minor buildings. In the 1240s David de Burnham, Bishop of St Andrews consecrated many churches in his diocese, which encompassed much of Fife and Lothian. A good number of these have surviving features likely to be of c1220-40, as at Arbuthnott and Burntisland. Both these have separate chancels, as does Preston in Borders. Other churches of this period at Cowie, Cullen, Mortlach and Rattray in NE Scotland, and Barevan in Highland are single chambers. Cowie and Rattray have triple east east lancets, and other triple lancet sets remain at Allangrange, Kilmacolm, and Preston in Lothian. Chapels near the castles of Dunstaffnage and Skipness are the largest and finest 13th century churches on the west coast, where modest size, simplicity and conservatism were the norm. There even in the late medieval period openings were often either still round-arched or crudely made slits covered with lintel slabs rather than arched over .

East end of the chancel at Kilmacolm

Blocked doorway at Kincardine

St Blane's Church, Isle of Bute, showing the 13th century east end

The Scots' struggle for independence from English rule and the ravages of the Black Death gave little impetus to the construction of fine churches on the mainland during the first two thirds of the 14th century. Amongst parish churches The single chamber at Temple and the chancel at Douglas are the only noteworthy structures of that period. Of the last third of the 14th century are parts of an aisled nave and transepts at St Giles at Edinburgh, the west tower at Inverkeithing, a single chamber with a vestry on one side at Maybole, a vaulted chancel with a vestry at Bothwell, and a central tower, transepts and vaulted chancel at St Monans. The latter three churches served colleges of priests set up to pray for the souls of deceased members of the nobility and the royal family. Such colleges were known in Scotland by the late 13th century but they became particularly fashionable in the 15th and early 16th centuries. Eventually there were about forty of them Scotland, both in urban and rural areas. Only at Aberdeen, Edinburgh and St Andrews were there medieval colleges in the modern sense of the word as seats of learning with lots of young students. Chapels that served them still remain. Other college chapels eventually came to serve as parish churches, although some were originally private chapels additional to the parochial system, such as Seton and Roslin. In towns colleges were created by grouping together all the regular clergy and the extra priests who served the various chantry chapels in a church.

Most parish churches were founded by lay lords, sometimes as a condition of being given as estate. Teinds or a tenth of the produce of all land was set aside to support each church and its rector or parson. By the late medieval period most churches had been piously handed over by lay lords and put under the control of a monastery or a cathedral or some other religious body, which took most of the teind, the services often being conducted by poorly paid vicars. This was one reason why most rural churches in Scotland remained modest both in size and detail. Only in the burghs were there laymen with the money, inclination and enough power over the running of their local church to allow the addition of aisles, porches, vestries and towers.

Temple Church

Window at Covington

The building of the splendid new chancel with aisles the same height as the main body at St Giles at Edinburgh in the early 15th century marked the beginning of a boom period for church construction in the southern and central parts of Scotland which continued until the 1540s. A splendid new collegiate church at Lincluden was begun at the same time by the Douglases to replace a decayed nunnery that had recently suppressed. In the mid 15th century the burgh churches of Perth and Haddington were rebuilt with fully aisled naves and chancels divided by central towers with transepts. Stirling and Linlithgow also have fully aisled cruciform churches, but with the apsed east ends added in the early 16th century and towers located at the west end. Only the west tower remains of a large cruciform church at Dundee and not much more of another at St Andrews. Dalkeith is also aisled and cruciform although the apsed choir is aisleless. Polygonal apses also occur in college chapels at Edinburgh and St Andrews, and in churches at Aberdeen, Biggar, Castle Semple, Ladykirk, Midcalder and Seton.

Rodel on Harris has a small but unusually complete cruciform 16th century church with a tall west tower. The only other parish church with a tower anywhere in the western Highlands and Islands was Kilmun in Argyll. Slightly larger cruciform churches with central towers are at Crichton, Dunglass and Whitekirk. Small west towers occur at the early 16th century churches of Castle Semple and Ladykirk (Borders). Both these have east apses and Ladykirk also has a pair of apsidal-ended transepts. The only other such transepts were single ones in the parish church at Arbuthnott and at a friary church at St Andrews. Ladykirk in Ayrshire has a tiny south transeptal tower. Dalserf has a plan which is unique in Scotland, being a long fully aisled rectangle with a lofty tower set over the western bay of the south aisle. St Vigeans also ended up as a rather shorter fully aisled rectangle with a west tower. Muthil was a rare Scottish example of a more typically English plan with an aisled nave with the tower engaged by the aisles and an unaisled chancel. Late medieval single chamber churches remain fairly complete at Covington, Fowlis Easter, Fowlis Wester, Grandtully, Innerpeffray and Tain.

St Mary's Church, Haddington

Construction of the larger churches usually stretched the available resources to the limit. Often there were several separate campaigns, parts such as transepts often being added later, as at Seton and Tullibardine. At Rosslyn a fully aisled and vaulted choir with the most sumptuous all-over decoration of the piers and surfaces was completed along with the eastern walls of transepts upon which no further work was ever completed and no nave was ever begun. The large burgh church at Stirling lacked the intended transepts right up until the early 20th century. Many other churches were never finished as originally intended. Corstophine ended up with a chancel wider and higher than the older nave, which was never replaced, to which are attached a west tower and a SW transept. At St Monans any plan to build a nave was soon abandoned.

Old postcard of the church of the Holy Rude at Stirling

Remains of vaulting, St Martin's Church, Haddington

Linlithgow Church

With their thick walls, vaults, and windows with flowing tracery, late medieval Scottish parish churches are distinctively different from those of England. The loop-tracery of c1500 in windows at Dalkeith, Linlithgow, Seton, Stow and Tullibardine has parallels in Ireland and France but not in England or Wales. In lesser Scottish churches windows were small and often simply arched or square headed with minimal tracery (if any at all), and where tracery does occur it adopts what in England would be regarded as archaic forms such as the intersecting tracery at Tain, the geometrical forms in the transept at Straiton, and the floral based designs at Covington, Linlithgow and Seton. Linlithgow comes closest to the English late medieval ideal with its lofty arcades, low clerestory and independently-gabled side chapels rather than true transepts.

Highland churches often had thatched roofs but Lowland churches were covered with either sheets of lead, slates, or huge flat slabs set over vaults which necessitated very thick walls, as at Whitekirk. Some of the vaults have decorative ribs as at Ladykirk, Rosslyn and Seton; genuine rib-vaults often occurred in abbeys and cathedrals but in parish churches only tend to appear over aisles, porches and towers rather than over the wide span of the main body. Stone vaults made churches less vulnerable to arson during raids. Crow-stepped gables are a feature peculiar to Scotland. Such gables and parapets were sometimes supported on fine mouldings. Piers were sometimes circular as at Stirling, and the round arch came back into fashion. Burgh churches at Dundee Haddington and St Andrews have processional twin round-arched west doorways set under a wide semi-circular arch. The towers at Ayr and Dalserf resemble contemporary secular tower houses with gabled caphouses over the tops of the spiral stairs. St Giles at Edinburgh has a fine crown-spire. Only about fifty Scottish churches ever had a tower during the medieval period, most of them in towns and in villages along the east coast. Other churches had a bellcote to house one or two bells perched on the west gable as at Kinneil, although few genuine medieval examples still survive in Scotland. The collegiate churches usually have sedilia or seats for priests on the south side near the altar, together with a piscina. A feature found in several of the simple rectangular churches in Aberdeenshire and Moray is a sacrament house or decorative cupboard to contain the consecrated host, good examples being at Cullen, Deskford and Kinkell.

From the mid 15th century it became common practice for a local laird to add a transept to a church as a burial place and chantry chapel. Transeptal chapels were known in Scotland as aisles and should not be confused with aisles of a more longi-tudinal type added to provide extra width to a nave. Transeptal aisles often remained in use after the ruination or replacement of the rest of the church, as at Banff, Carn-wath, Dalry, Edzell, Fordyce, Guthrie and Methven. They continued to be built after the Reformation and enabled lairds to ignore a decree of 1581 forbidding burials within churches. The later ones often had two levels, with an elevated family pew set over a dark and low burial vault. After the Reformation chancels were often walled off and remodelled as burial vaults, with or without a family pew above. This would ensure their survival in the period between the late 16th and late 19th centuries when chancels were not a ritual requirement and were often demolished, or in the case of large aisled examples in burghs, used as quite separate churches with their own congregations.

Churches normally had the east end (or the chancel if there was one) divided off by a screen, usually of wood, upon which was mounted a rood or crucifix. Zealous reformers or ruination caused the loss of all the early ones but a 16th century example remains at Fowlis Easter. Even in single-celled churches the position of the former screen is often indicated by the window layout since direct sunlight was required upon the screen and any altars against it. Sometimes the rood was mounted on just a plain single beam. Otherwise it was put on a loft set over the screen which could used by musicians and actors. Plays could an important means of conveying the message of Biblical stories in an age when services contained masses in Latin not readily under-standable by common folk. Wall paintings served the same purpose but Reformers usually obliterated them under coats of whitewash and plaster, so they rarely survive in Scottish churches. Medieval church furnishings are rare in Scotland. Little survives of the many fine stained glass windows smashed by Reformers. Old doors or pews with carved figures or other motifs now rarely survive either. Twenty old fonts remain, but most of them are plain or very damaged, except those at Inverkeithing and Meigle.

Transeptal burial chapel at Guthrie

Sedilia at St Monans

Doorway at Tain

Cockburnspath Church

For a few decades after the Reformation of 1559-60 most of the existing stock of churches remained in use, although carefully scraped clean of altars, images of saints and anything else that hinted at Catholicism. Parts of monastic churches and cathedrals sometimes served for parochial worship in the medieval period. Reformed services required smaller spaces and with a requirement for everyone to see (and be seen from) the pulpit. Large churches were subdivided for use by more than one congregation (as seen at Aberdeen and Dundee), or the surplus parts were demolished. Many mainland churches were rebuilt or replaced in the late 16th century and the 17th century. Others were abandoned for a new church built elsewhere, as at Burntisland. The 19th century also saw the replacement of many ancient churches. Currently less than half of the places in Scotland which once had a medieval church or chapel still have recognisable standing remains of the main body of whatever stood in that period. Including eight former cathedrals and a dozen monastic churches about seventy five Scottish churches still have a medieval main body which is still roofed. Only about sixty of those are regularly still in use for services, a third of them being in Lothian.

Doorway at Maison Dieu at Brechin

Dunglass Church

As a result of the combined ravages of reformers, restorers and ruination only a few of the churches described in this book now have fully three-dimensional monumental effigies earlier than the 1560s. Empty tomb recesses hint at many lost monuments, although not all of them contained three-dimensional effigies. Most of the surviving effigies are 15th or 16th century knights, occasionally with wives. Lone female effigies remain at Airth and Lincluden, ecclesiastics at Bathgate and St Andrews, and a rare example of an earl in civilian dress with his wife at Dalkeith. Only in the late medieval period was it common for land owners to be buried in parish churches. Previously those of high rank tended to be buried in the monastic churches or cathedrals of which they were benefactors. Effigies so located are described in the companion book on abbeys and cathedrals. In the parish churches the only early effigies are the priest of c1200 at Bathgate and 13th century knight at Arbuthnott.

Corstophine has three effigies of 15th century knights and there are two at Douglas. Rodel has three effigies of 16th century knights and there is another at Fordyce. Other effigies of note are at Borthwick, Ceres, Rothesay, and Seton. Several places in Argyll such as Keills and Kilmartin have collections of late medieval military effigies in half-relief that are so numerous that some of them may have been outside the churches. Some of these effigies are quite small but one at Eye in the Western Isles is life-sized. Lasswade in Lothian had an effigy of this type and there is another depicting a couple at Kildrummy. Grave-slabs with crosses, parts of inscriptions and low-relief motifs such as swords, galleys, and chalices are common in Argyll and the Western Isles. There are also a few slabs where an effigy is created by incised lines. Examples are the knights at Kinkell and Rosslyn, couples at Longforgan and Rossie, and priests at St Andrews and Tranent. The same idea was also used on sheets of brass, but the metal was too valuable to be left lying around in churches, especially ones falling into ruin, and the three Scottish brasses now surviving in situ are all of after 1560.

Post-reformation effigies are not all that common either as a result of the ban imposed on burial in churches in 1581. Wall tablets with ornate frames, long inscriptions sometimes in rhyme, plus heraldry, and emblems of death, rank or an occupation became the norm from the late 16th century onwards.

Tomb at Dalkeith showing an earl in civilian dress

Low-relief effigies at Kildrummy

The tomb at Borthwick

Tomb recess at Tain

Effigy of a knight at Aberdeen

Effigy of a priest at Bathgate

Tomb on the north side of the chancel at Rothesay

Abercorn Church, showing the later burial places grouped around a 12th century core

GAZETTEER OF MEDIEVAL SCOTTISH CHURCHES

ABDIE   Fife   *St Magridin*   NO 260164   By Lindores Loch, 3km SE of Newburgh

The chancel with its pilaster buttresses and lancets, with a group of three in the east wall must date from about the time of the consecration in 1242 by David de Bernham, Bishop of St Andrews. The more thinly walled nave with the same external width as the chancel and a further series of shallow buttresses is also 13th century. All appearing to be 17th century work are the more boldly projecting buttresses and porch on the south side, the transeptal Denmylne Aisle of 1661 on the north side, the bellcote on the west gable and monuments to the Adamson, Balfour, Spens and Thomstone families.

ABERCORN   Lothian   NT 082792   4km W of Forth Bridge

There was an early monastery here and a bishop's see existed by 685. Most of the single long narrow body forming the nave and chancel is of 1579, but on the nave south side is a blocked 12th century doorway with shafts, chevrons on the arch, and a tympanum with a lozenge pattern. Most of the chancel was taken over as the Hopetoun family pew in 1708. They also added a retiring room on the north which is set over a vault which contains fragments of two 8th century crosses, two hogback grave-stones, two 13th century coffin lids and various other sculptured fragments. The Duddingston aisle dated 1612 lies south of the chancel, and the Binns aisle and vault of 1618 lie in a south transeptal position. The north aisle with its three bay arcade and the west front and chancel arch all date from the restoration of 1893.

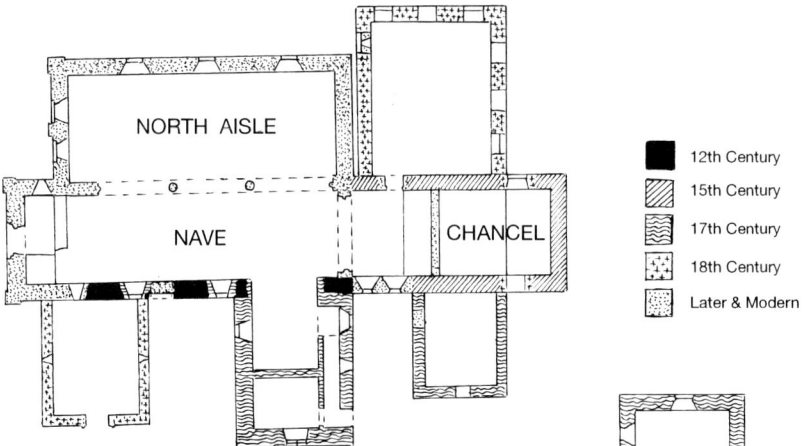

■	12th Century
▨	15th Century
▧	17th Century
⊡	18th Century
⬚	Later & Modern

Plan of Abercorn Church

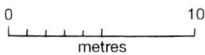

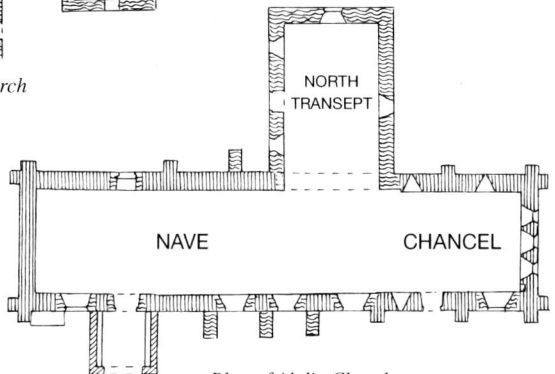

0   10
metres

Plan of Abdie Church

ABERDEEN Aberdeenshire *St Nicholas* NJ 931064 Just west of city centre

This was the largest medieval parish church in Scotland, once 75m long, and is first mentioned in a Bull of Pope Adrian IV in 1157. The footings of an apse recently found under the floor just east of the crossing must have belonged to a building already a generation or two old by then. Latterly the church was served by a college of 30 chaplains under a provost. Of the medieval building there remain the rib-vaulted chapel of St Mary (Our Lady of Pity) under the east end and the late 12th century piers of the crossing tower, plus the much refaced transepts of sandstone rubble with round-arched windows, still original internally. The crossing replaced the chancel of the early 12th century church. The south transept appears to have been lengthened in the late medieval period and was refaced externally in 1836-8. It contains a brass inscription to Alexander Irvine of Drum, d1457 and his wife Elizabeth de Keith. The north transept has a large blocked east arch of c1190-1210 towards the former north chapel beside the chancel. St Mary's Chapel was built c1430-35 by Lady Elizabeth Gordon as a mortuary for her family and lay under the fifth bay and the polygonal apse of the chancel finally begun in 1477. In the chapel was buried Sir John Gordon of Findlater after he was executed in 1562 following defeat by Queen Mary's forces at Corrichie.

From 1605 onwards, when an unofficial General Assembly of the Scottish Kirk was held here despite the protests of James VI (by then down in England), the transepts and crossing served as a vestibule to two separate churches in the former nave and chancel. The latter was rebuilt as a galleried aisle-less room 1834 and again in 1874 after a fire caused the wooden spire of 1513 on the central tower to fall upon it. James Gibbs designed the Classical style new western church of 1751-5 which is 5m shorter than the nine bay long 13th century nave and aisles with a west front of 1537-41 that it replaced. The old nave had been abandoned as unsafe in 1732 and parts of the arcades collapsed ten years later, the ruins being used in 1746 as a provender store for the Duke of Cumberland's cavalry. The west church contains monuments to Provost Robert Davidson, who was killed defending the city against the Lord of the Isles in 1411, Marjory Lidel, wife of Gilbert Menzies, c1460, Provost John Colliston, c1450, his wife Margaret Seton, Provost Menzies, d1641, and a large brass plate to the noted 17th scholar Dr Duncan Liddel.

Crypt chapel at St Nicholas' Church, Aberdeen

King's College Chapel at Aberdeen

The crossing arches at Aberdeen

King's College, forming the heart of the University between the city centre and the former cathedral of St Machar to the north, was founded by Bishop Elphinstone in the 1490s and has a chapel of that period with a tower with a crown-spire which was rebuilt in 1633. The remains of Elphinstone's tomb lie beside a pulpit of 1627 brought here from the cathedral. The chapel west end is screened off as a war memorial.

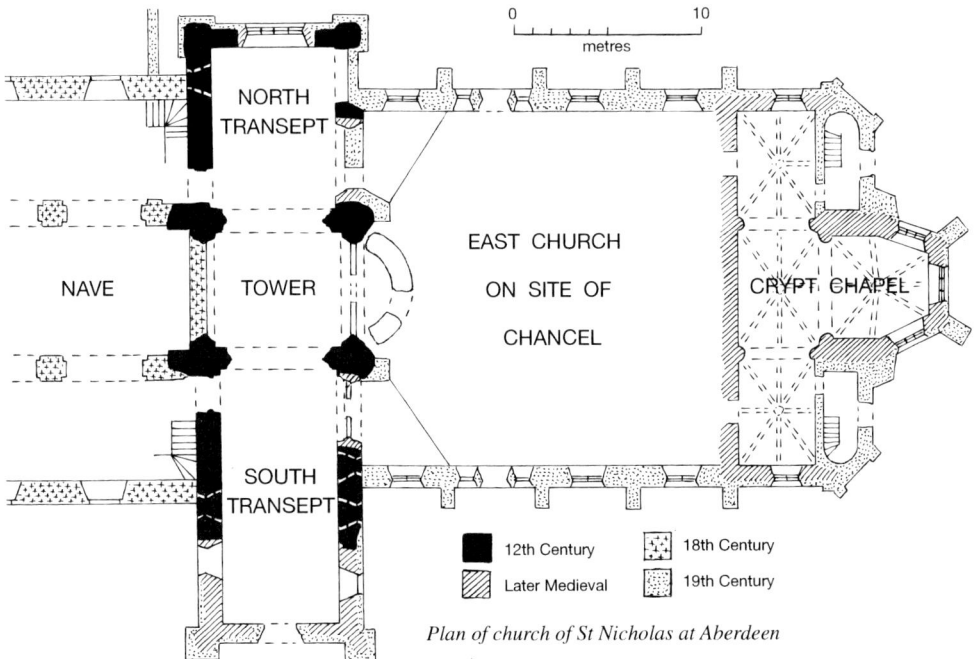

0   10
metres

NORTH TRANSEPT

NAVE   TOWER

EAST CHURCH
ON SITE OF
CHANCEL

CRYPT CHAPEL

SOUTH TRANSEPT

■ 12th Century   ▨ 18th Century

▨ Later Medieval   ▨ 19th Century

Plan of church of St Nicholas at Aberdeen

Aberdour Church

ABERDOUR   Fife   *St Fillan*   NT 194855   Just to the east of the castle ruins

The nave with one original NE window and the chancel with four restored original windows are both 12th century, with an arch of that period between them. The south aisle with its three bay arcade and porch are of c1500-10, although the aisle windows are all modern. The transeptal Phin aisle on the north was added in 1608.

ABERLADY   Lothian   *St Mary*   NT 462798   11km SW of North Berwick

The 15th century west tower has a recessed top storey and a slated spire behind a corbelled parapet. Part of it once served as a dovecot. Two burial aisles of c1600 have been incorporated into the north side of the main building of 1886 which has an aisle duplicating them on the south side and small porches set on either side of the tower. There is a replica of a fragment (now in the National Museum of Antiquities) of an 8th century cross-shaft carved with part of an angel and a panel with intertwined birds.

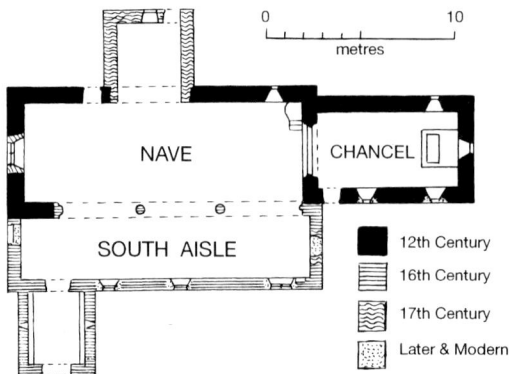

Plan of Aberdour Church

Aberlady Church

ABERNETHY   Perth & Kinross   NO 190165   10km SE of Perth

Nothing remains of a medieval church here, which became Scotland's second collegiate church in 1328, but a relic of an early Celtic monastery here is the late 11th century round tower 22m high and 4.5m diameter at the base, where there is a Pictish slab adorned with a tuning-fork, hammer, crescent and a V-rod.

AIRTH   Falkirk   NS 901869   South end of Airth, 7km north of Falkirk

The blocked arch into the Bruce burial aisle of 1614 is actually the surviving easternmost arch of a late 12th century three bay arcade to a north aisle. The circular pier has a waterleaf capital. On the south side is an ashlar-faced transeptal chapel built c1460-80 by Alexander Bruce of Airth which contains a female effigy of c1330. West of it is a laird's aisle dated 1593 on the gable with initials of Alexander Elphinstone and his wife Janet Livingstone, inside which are several heraldic grave slabs of that period. The east end of 1647 has on the south side a tower-porch built against the Airth aisle and on the north side is an aisle with a three bay arcade of round arches set on round-cornered piers. The nave west wall is also of that period.

ALTYRE   Moray   NJ 036554   3km south of Forres

This ruin of 1300 has a two-light east window now lacking its Y-tracery and a pair of opposed doorways with round rere-arches. A screen once divided the church between the pairs of lancets in the north and south walls.

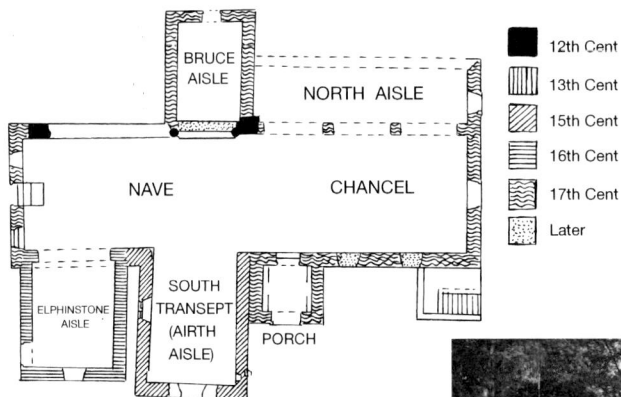

Abernethy Round Tower

Plan of Airth Church

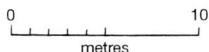

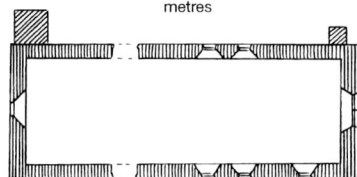

Plan of Altyre Church

Altyre Church

ALYTH Perth & Kinross *St Molluag* NO 246484 At SE end of the town

All that remains of the church are an arcade of three wide bays between the wide nave and the north aisle added c1500, and the chancel north wall in line with the arcade in which is a round-headed window perhaps of c1200. There is also a sacrement-house now obscured by a monument and a blocked doorway leads through to the site of a 15th century north chapel with two south aumbries, one of them triangular headed.

ANSTRUTHER Fife *St Adrian* NO 564036 In middle of Anstruther Wester

A 16th century tower with pairs of round-headed belfry windows and a slated broach spire within a balustraded parapet lies at the west end of a short but wide church of 1846 which once served Anstruther Wester. The church at Anstruther Easter is of the 1630s, when a new parish was created by dividing off part of that of Kilrenny.

ARBUTHNOTT Aberdeenshire *St Ternan* NO 801746 4km NW of Inverbervie

Little altered since it was consecrated in 1242 by Bishop David de Bernham of St Andrews is the chancel with three east lancets and two on each of the north and south sides. Projecting south from it is the barrel-vaulted Arbuthnott aisle of c1500 which ends in a polygonal apse with lancets and corner buttresses and contains the 13th century effigy of Hugh Arbuthnott set on a 16th century tomb chest. The aisle has a cobbled floor and a crypt below. A staircase in the chapel NW corner leads to an upper room over the vault. Most of the nave is now mid 19th century and of after a fire in 1890, but some 13th century work may survive in the opposed north and south doorways. The west end with diagonal buttresses and a polygonal bell-turret is of c1500.

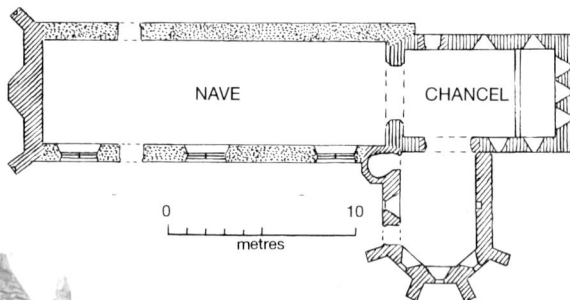

Plan of Arbuthnott Church

Arbuthnott Church

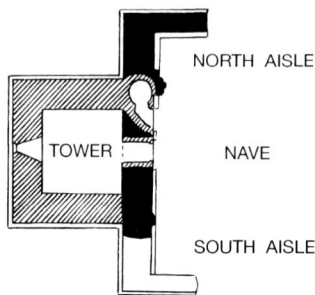

Plan of Ayr Church

St John's Church, Ayr

Barevan Church

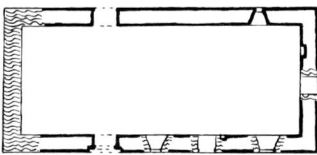

Plan of Auchindoir Church

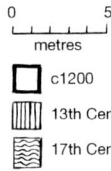

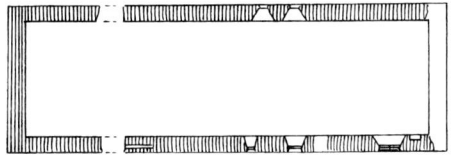

0   5
metres

☐ c1200

▥ 13th Cent

▨ 17th Cent

Plan of Barevan Church

AUCHINDOIR   Aberdeenshire   *St Mary*   NJ 477246   14km south of Huntly

This attractively sited ruin has two good opposed round-headed doorways of c1200 and one original north lancet with a round rere-arch. The west wall, east doorway and the south windows are 17th century. The south doorway has a finely moulded arch with a dog-tooth frieze on the hoodmould and shafts with waterleaf capitals. See p1.

AYR   Strathclyde   *St John*   NS 334222   On north side of the tower, towards river

The late 12th century church had an aisled nave with arcades of two orders of round arches and a total external width of 13m. Of it there remains only the west wall with the respond of the north arcade. The west window now looks into an ashlar-faced 15th century tower at the summit of which is a corbel table supporting a parapet with roundels and a gabled caphouse over the spiral-staircase in the NE corner. The church lay within the outer defences of a castle built by King William the Lion in 1202, but which were not restored after being dismantled c1310. A large new Cromwellian fort was built in 1652 around the church, which then served as an armoury. The Protector donated 200 merks towards construction of a more conveniently sited new church elsewhere.

BAREVAN   Highland   *St Aibind*   NH 837473   S of Cawdor, 16km E of Inverness

This 13th century church has been a ruin since a more conveniently sited new church was built at Cawdor in 1619. The pair of north lancets probably lay on either side of a screen. Two south windows here are more widely spaced and further east is a two-light window with Y-tracery. There are opposed north and south doorways (the latter with a drawbar slot) in the nave, and a narrower priest's doorway on the south side further east. Little remains of the end walls but there were probably triple east lancets. Much of the floor is formed of old graveslabs.

BARHOBBLE Dumfries & Galloway NX 310494 14km SW of Wigtown

Remains of a mid 12th century church here were only recognised as such a few decades ago. Clay was used to bond the stone walls rather than mortar. Crucks carrying the roof divided the interior into three bays, the eastern one having a screen below it. After being damaged by fire c1200 the church was downgraded to a chapel in favour of a new church at Mochrum and a priest's room took the place of the western bay.

BARRA Western Isles *St Barr* NF 706074 At the north end of Barra

This is a rare Scottish example of a grouping of small churches and chapels, typical of early monastic sites in Ireland. The 12th century church of St Barr has a round-arched north doorway and three round-headed windows with triangular rere-arches. The east wall is broken down. The 15th century chapel to the SE has a window with an arched head cut in a lintel. To the NE is a 16th century chapel which has been re-roofed to protect four late medieval grave-slabs and a cast of a 10th century slab with runes.

BASSENDEAN Borders *St Mary* NT 631457 15km NW of Kelso

This was originally a 12th century chapel held by the nuns of Coldstream Priory. It later became a parish church and in the 16th century was rebuilt as a single chamber with the south wall containing a lintelled doorway, two windows (one of two lights) and a piscina. There is no east window and an aumbry is the only feature in the north wall. After closure in 1649 the church was adapted as an open burial enclosure of the Homes. It contains a medieval cross-slab and a crudely made font or stoup.

BATHGATE Lothian NS 990681 2km ESE of the town centre

Of c1200 are the small NE lancet and the north doorway jambs with worn stiffleaf capitals on the short missing shafts. At least one jamb has been moved to widen the doorway since the church was abandoned in 1739. There is a weathered half-relief type effigy of a 13th century priest and a slab to Andrew Crichton of Drumcorse, d1502.

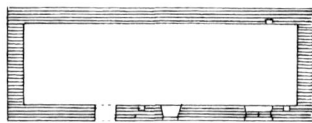

Plan of Bassendean Church

16th Century
Later & Modern

Lancet at Bathgate

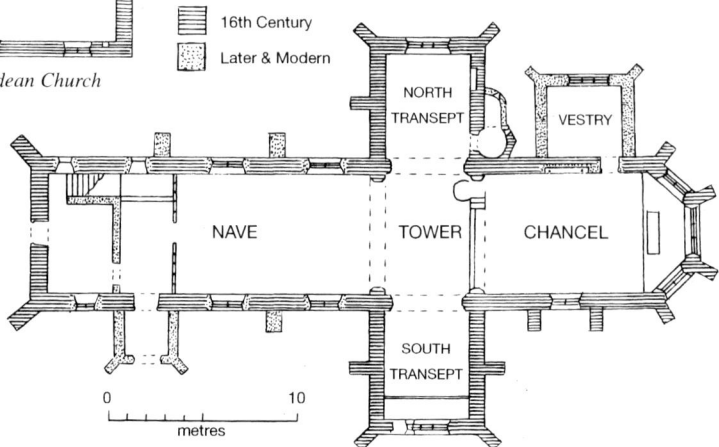

NORTH TRANSEPT
VESTRY
NAVE
TOWER
CHANCEL
SOUTH TRANSEPT

0   10
metres

Plan of Biggar Church

Old postcard of Biggar Church

BIGGAR   Lanarkshire *St Mary* NT 040379 On the north side of the town

The ashlar-faced central tower, the diagonally buttressed transepts with windows just in the end walls, and the three bay long chancel with a buttressed polygonal apse date from the time of the establishment of a college here by the Fleming family in 1545. The chancel has original windows of two and three lights. The tower is rectangular rather than square and has a polygonal staircase turret and a gunport in each side of the parapet. The rubble-built nave with diagonal corner buttresses and west and south doorways is also 16th century. The pointed-headed windows set in square frames are 19th century, as are the south porch and north vestry, plus all the stained glass making the interior rather dark. The west end of the nave is now divided off. See back cover.

BIRNIE   Grampian *St Brandon*

NJ 207588   4km SSW of Elgin

The see of Moray was located here from 1107 to 1184 and the nave and smaller chancel and the arch between them are all of that period, although they seem too modest to have served as a cathedral. There is no east window, the chancel having small round-headed windows facing north and south. Over the priest's doorway is a damaged 14th century window. The nave has plain opposed doorways, that on the north now blocked. The three south windows and probably the west wall are of 1734. See photo on page 4.

Plan of Birnie Church

Birnie Church

BIRSAY   Orkney   *St Magnus*   HY 248277   At the NW end of Mainland

The church has tiny blocked 13th century lancets on each side and a small blocked round-headed north doorway. The birdcage bellcote probably dates from 1664 and the building was enlarged in 1760. It has a late medieval font bearing the Tulloch or Craigie arms. Footings of an 11th and 12th century chancel have been found outside the east wall. Earl Thorfinn built a minster here c1115-20. It was briefly a cathedral until 1137. For the church of Brough of Birsay see Medieval Abbeys and Cathedrals of Scotland.

BORTHWICK   Lothian   *St Kentigern*   NT 369596   9km SEE of Dalkeith

Much of the church, including the NW tower, north transept and vestries is of 1862, but the apse and the chancel south wall are relics of a mostly 12th century church destroyed by fire in 1775. On the north side the Dundas of Arniston burial aisle incorporates parts of a late medieval sacristy with a piscina and traces of east and west windows, its doorway from the chancel now blocked. On the south side is a south transeptal chapel probably built in the 1440s by William, first Lord Borthwick, whose arms appear on the gable. Buttresses on the east and west sides help carry the weight of the stone flagged roof over the pointed tunnel-vault. There is a damaged piscina on the south side and a stoup beside the west doorway of the 1860s. Outside is an eaves cornice with foliage and grotesque heads. Set against the windowless east wall of the chapel is a fine tomb with effigies of Lord Borthwick and his wife (see p15). Until 1862 this tomb lay within the apse but it may have originally been located somewhere else.

BOTHWELL   Lanarkshire   *St Bride*   NS 705586   In the middle of the town

The large four-bay chancel with a slab-roof over a vault supported by buttresses between windows of two and three lights is a relic of a college founded in the 1390s by Archibald the Grim, Earl of Douglas. It has a north vestry and contains 17th and 18th century monuments. The existing aisled nave with a west porch, transepts and a central tower is of 1833. In 1933 the old and new parts were finally connected and traces of a 12th century chancel were found.

Borthwick Church

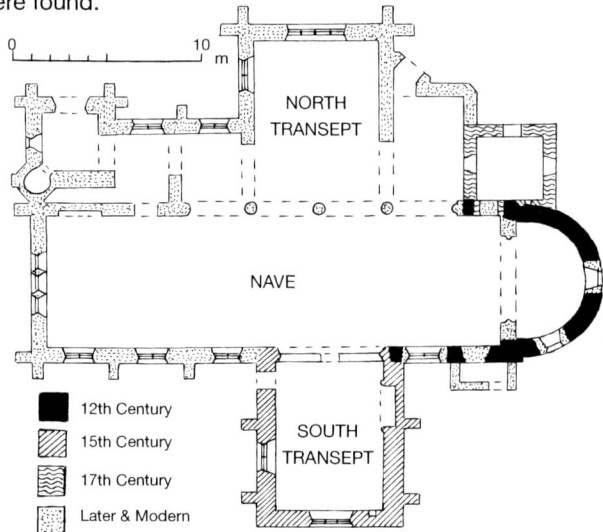

Plan of Borthwick Church

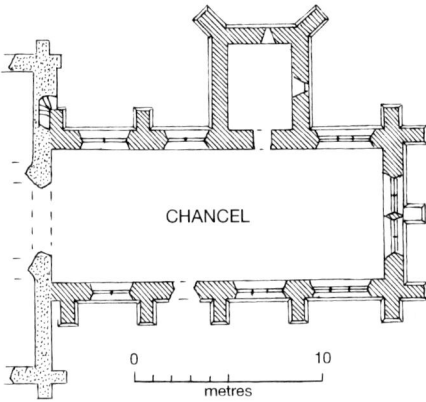

Plan of collegiate chancel at Bothwell

Collegiate chancel at Bothwell

BOWDEN   Borders   NT 554303   4km south of Melrose

The main body has a blocked round-arched north doorway and 12th century walling on the west and north sides, it having been one of David I's endowments of the abbey of Selkirk (later moved to Kelso) The taller Roxburghe aisle of 1644 with a loft with an external stair set over a vault added at the east end now forms the chancel, and the aisle on the north side dated 1661 with a loft and vault of the Kers of Cavers now contains the organ, the fine laird's pew having been moved further east in a remodelling of 1908, from which dates most of the south side with its doorway and five windows.

BRECHIN   Angus   NO 600602   In town centre.

The south wall containing a shafted doorway and three finely moulded lancets is all that remains of a 13th century chapel known as Maison Dieu which served a hospital. See Medieval Abbeys and Cathedrals of Scotland for the round tower and the cathedral, which has always served as the parish church. See picture on page 13.

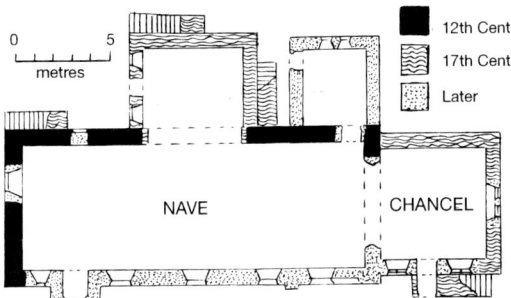

	12th Cent
	17th Cent
	Later

Plan of Bowden Church

The Maison Dieu at Brechin

Buittle Church

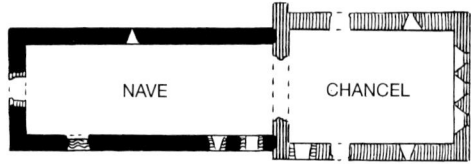

Plan of Buittle Church

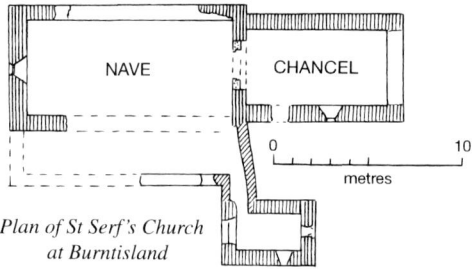

Plan of St Serf's Church at Burntisland

BUITTLE Dumfries & Galloway *St Colman* NX 808599 3km SW of Dalbeattie

The 12th century nave has one original window in the leaning north wall and a blocked doorway on the south side. The west doorway is 13th century and the small south window and doorway near it are 17th century, whilst the bellcote on the west gable is of 1745. A good double-chamfered arch leads through to a late 13th century chancel rather wider than the nave. It has a doorway and a lancet with a shouldered rere-arch in each of the north and south walls (though the latter is partly rebuilt, and three east lancets with segmental rere-arches with a doorway of the 1740s below the middle one.

BURNTISLAND Fife *St Serf* NT 233864 On north side of the town

The medieval church lies in the middle of a housing estate and was abandoned after a new church elsewhere was completed in 1600. It is essentially the building consecrated by the bishop of St Andrews in 1242. Of the nave only the west gable with a lancet in it still stands high. The sharply pointed chancel arch lies on simple imposts. The east lancets have gone but one lancet and the priest's doorway in the south wall still remain. To the south is a tiny 13th century chapel, once vaulted and intended to house a holy relic or mark the site of an early chapel. A 15th century aisle joining it to the nave has been mostly destroyed.

St Serf's Church at Burtisland

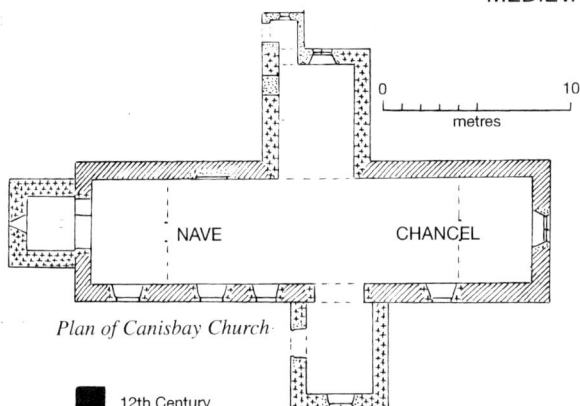

Plan of Canisbay Church

12th Century
13th Century
15th Century
17th Century
18th Century
Later & Modern

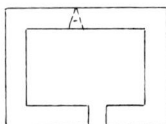

Bute: St Ninian's

St Blane's Church, Bute

NAVE   CHANCEL

Plan of St Blane's Church on Bute

Canisbay Church

BUTE   Isle of Bute   *St Blane*   NS 095534   Towards the south end of the island

Outside the present churchyard at St Blane's drystone walls of a hut known as the Devil's Cauldron are probably remains of the monastery established here possibly as early as the 6th century. Footings of a rectangular chapel lie by the western wall of the lower part of the graveyard. Similar drystone chapels on Bute remain at St Ninian's (033612), where traces of a north window remain, and Kilmichael (NR 991705), which is orientated south-north and has an aumbry and an altar with a relic recess (see p4). Chapels with more meagre remains are at Cruiksland (037627) and St Mary's (045595).

On the upper part of the graveyard at St Blane's low ashlar walls remain of a 12th century nave with opposed doorways and western pilaster buttresses. Better preserved is the chancel arch with chevrons and dog-tooth. The west part of the chancel with a south doorway and adjacent window is also 12th century. The eastern part with two east lancets, another lancet facing north and a wider south window is late 13th century. Many 12th and 13th slabs lie within and around the church.

There is a separate entry for the church of St Mary at Rothesay on page 80.

CANISBAY   Highland   *St Drostan*   NT 344729   23km north of Wick

The long main body with a SW doorway blocked up and hidden under harling in 1891 represents the much rebuilt 15th century church. The west tower was added in 1704. The south transept dated 1724 was converted to a porch in 1891. The north transept was added in 1736 and the date 1720 appears on a skewputt on the nave.

Cardross Church

Transeptal chapel at Carnwath

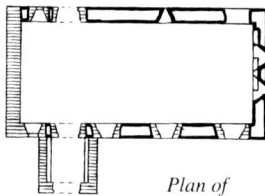

Plan of Carnock Church

☐	c1200 - 20
▨	14th Century
▩	15th Century
▤	16th Century
▨	Later & Modern

0   10
└─┴─┴─┴─┴─┴─┴─┴─┴─┴─┘ m

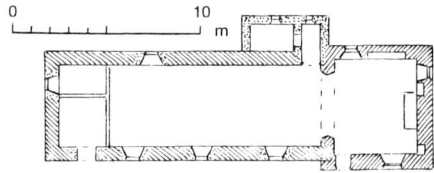

Plan of Cardross Church

CARDROSS   Dumbartonshire   *St Mahew*   NS 393750   6km NW of Dumbarton

The nave may go back to David II's reign when the church was a chapel-of-ease to a church at Rosneath but its features are all much later, with sash-windows. The short but wider and taller chancel with stepped gables and a fine sacrament house in the north wall probably dates from a rebuilding by Duncan Napier prior to a reconsecration in 1467. In 1640 it was walled off as a burial aisle and the nave became a school, the two parts only being re-roofed and re-connected again as one building in 1955.

CARNOCK   Fife   NT 041890   In Carnock, 5km WNW of Dunfermline

The small ruined church of c1200-20 has two lancets in the east wall and another facing north. In 1250 it was put by Bishop Bernham under the control of the Trinitarian friars of Scotlandwell. The round-arched and lintelled south windows and the south porch and west wall date from alterations and repairs recorded in 1602 and 1641. The 1602 work was sponsored by Sir George Bruce, whose initials appear on the SE skewputt. In the porch is what appears to be a damaged and reset medieval stoup.

CARNWATH   Lanarkshire   *St Mary*   NS 975465   11km ENE of Lanark

Beside the present church is a slab-roofed transept of two bays with diagonal and mid-wall buttresses. The northern bay has windows in each side wall and a doorway to the north, whilst the other bay has a blocked arch towards the site of the medieval nave. The transept was added after the church was made collegiate in 1425 by Thomas, 1st Lord Somerville. It contains the tomb of Hugh, Lord Somerville, d1549 and his wife Janet and many Lockhart memorials from the late 17th century onwards.

CASTLE SEMPLE   Renfrewshire   NT 375601   2km NW of Lochwinnoch

Now a monument in state care, this ruined collegiate church contains in the chancel north wall the a recess with a foiled arch over the tomb chest of its founder, John, 1st Lord Semple, killed at Flodden in 1513. It has a tiny west tower and an east apse in which are two-light windows of a rather unusual form. Several square-headed original windows also remain in the south wall along with two doorways. A doorway on the north side led to a sacristy behind the tomb recess.

CAVERS   Borders   *St Cuthbert*   NT 540155

In grounds of Cavers House 4km ENE of Hawick

The eastern part of long main body of the derelict church is 12th century, with one original window at the east end of the north wall. Most of the older part is now divided off by partitions, a loft over a burial vault having being created in the east end for the Douglases of Cavers. The western part has some later medieval walling but the north tran-septal burial aisle of the Eliots of Stobs is 17th century, the blocked west doorway is dated 1662, and the walls were raised and given new windows at a still later date. A south transeptal aisle of the Gledstanes of Cocklaw which was demolished in the mid 18th century may have originally been a late medieval chantry chapel.

Carnock Church

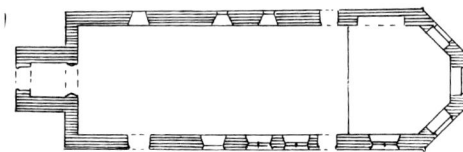

Plan of Castle Semple Church

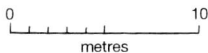

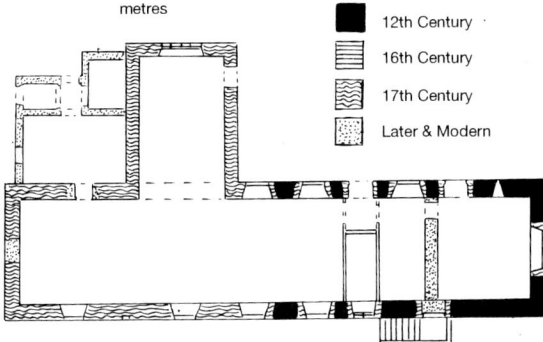

0   10
metres

■ 12th Century
▤ 16th Century
▨ 17th Century
▦ Later & Modern

Plan of Cavers Church

Tomb in Castle Semple Church

CHIRNSIDE   Borders   *St Fillan*   NT 870566   8km ENE of Duns

Original 12th century masonry remains in the lower parts of all four walls of the main block. Transferred from the nave south wall to the south side of a saddleback-roofed west tower of 1907 is a round-arched 12th century doorway with its inner order adorned with chevrons carried on engaged shafts with scalloped capitals. The outer order is roll-moulded and carried on free-standing shafts with cushion capitals. An older tower, probably late medieval and containing a vault, was taken down c1750. The transeptal north aisle of c1580-1625 was probably remodelled in 1703 and again in the 1830s, and much of the church is now of 1878 but with several additions of 1907.

COCKBURNSPATH   Borders   *St Helen*   NT 774711   In the middle of the village

The long main body of sandstone with a chamfered plinth and diagonal buttresses at all four corners is probably late medieval. Reset over the priest's doorway on the south side is the head of a late 13th or 14th century window with a quatrefoil between the heads of trefoiled lights. The small round tower straddling the middle of the west wall may be late 16th century but has a top stage of 1827. The ashlar faced burial vault at the east end was once dated 1614 with initials of William Arnot. The transeptal north aisle is probably of 1807 and most of the other features are late 19th century. This was a chapel-of-ease to Oldhamstocks originally, only becoming a parish church c1610.

Cockburnspath Church
See also page 13

▥	13th Cent
▨	15th Cent
▤	16th Cent
▦	Later

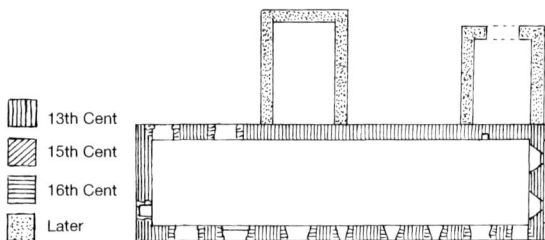

Plan of Cockpen Church

0   10
metres

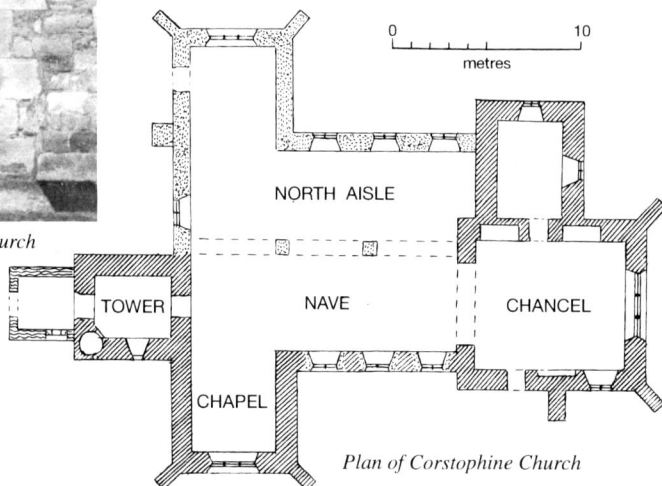

NORTH AISLE

TOWER   NAVE   CHANCEL

CHAPEL

Plan of Corstophine Church

Old print of Corstophine Church

COCKPEN   Lothian   NT 327633   4km south of Dalkeith

The east end of this ruin has remains of a 13th century circular window over a pair of lancets and corner pilasters. Excavations revealed footings of the original 12th century west wall removed when the building was later doubled in length probably in the early 14th century. Parts of a chevron-adorned 12th century arch were also found, along with evidence that the building lay ruinous for the second half of the 14th century. The many openings in the south wall all appear to be of after the Reformation.

CORSTOPHINE   Lothian   *St John Baptist*   NT 201728   6km west of Edinburgh

What is now the nave was originally a chantry chapel added c1390 by Sir Adam Forrester, several times Lord Provost of Edinburgh, to the south side of the pre-existing medieval parish church. The latter has been replaced by a north aisle of 1828 on the site of an older aisle of 1646 and the south windows are also of 1828. An effigy of Sir Adam, d1405, with his feet on a dog remains in a diagonally buttressed south-west transept with a good three light south window. There is also an old font from Gogar.

In 1429 the chantry chapel was made collegiate with a staff of five chaplains and two clerks, and another four chaplains were added in 1444. In the 1450s the chapel was given its own wider and taller chancel in the north wall of which are recesses with effigies of Sir John Forester, d1440, master of James I's household, and his son Sir John, c1454, with their wives. The latter lies under fine crocketed arch with angels carrying shields at the ends of the hood-mould. A doorway between the tombs leads to what was once a three storey sacristy. Other memorials here include slabs to Robert Heriot, Rector of Gogar, d1444 (with a chalice and wafer) and Alexander Tod, d1499, and the east wall has an inscription to Provost Nicholas Bannatyne who died in the 1470s. The chancel has bold diagonal corner buttresses, a three light east window with two lozenges in the tracery, and good set of sedilia with basket-arches and tiny rib-vaults. All parts of the church have slab-roofs over vaults, that of the nave only dating from 1903-5. The transept vault once had ribs set in a diamond pattern and its roof has a north gable so that it stands clear of the nave roof. The nave has its own west gable so that its roof does not connect with the west tower probably of the 1450s with a short stone spire with crenellated bands and pinnacles at the corners. The porch to the west of the tower is probably mid 17th century.

Cowie Church

Crail Church

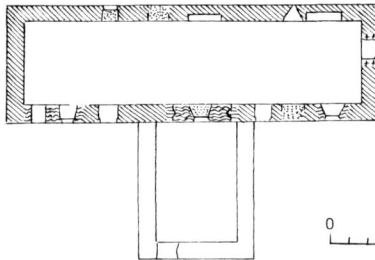

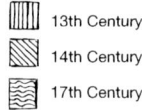

13th Century

14th Century

17th Century

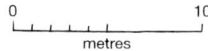

0   10

metres

Plan of Creich Church

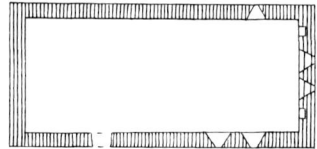

Plan of Craignish Chapel

COVINGTON   Lanarkshire   *St Michael*   NS 975398   10km SE of Lanark

In the blocking of the north doorway of this late medieval single chamber church is the date 1659 with the arms of the Lindsays of Covington Tower. On the south side are three original two-light windows with various types of tracery. A transeptal aisle has been added on the north side. A 12th century church is recorded here. See page 8.

COWIE   Aberdeenshire   *St Mary*   NO 884873   2km NE of Stonehaven

A chapel of St Nathalan once stood on this cliff-top site. The eastern two thirds of the present ruin, known in the 17th century as St Mary of the Storms, was built in 1276 by William Wishart, Bishop of St Andrews. It has three stepped lancets in the east gable and a 16th century priest's doorway on the south side. The western part is a poorly built late medieval extension and the side walls are mostly broken down.

CRAIGNISH   Argyll   *St Maelrubha*   NT 779154   6km WNW of Kilmartin

There are pairs of tomb slabs of c1500-60 on either side of the east end of a 13th century chapel with later medieval south doorway jambs. The windows are all towards the east end: two lancets in each of the east and south walls and one on the north.

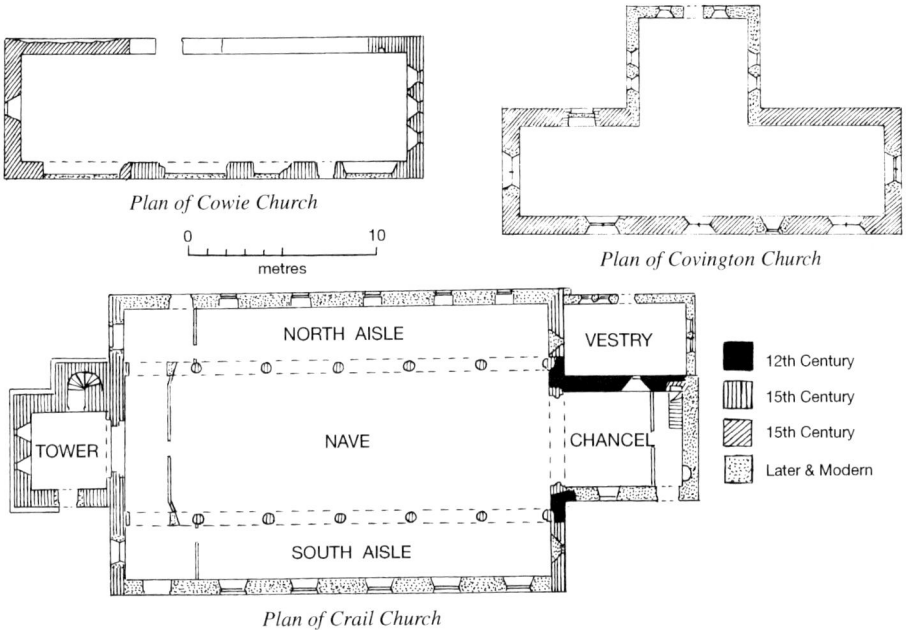

Plan of Cowie Church

0   10
metres

Plan of Covington Church

Plan of Crail Church

NORTH AISLE
VESTRY
TOWER
NAVE
CHANCEL
SOUTH AISLE

■ 12th Century
▥ 15th Century
▨ 15th Century
▦ Later & Modern

CRAIL   Fife   *St Mary*   NT 614089   At the north end of the town

The eastern corners of the nave and the chancel north wall with one window are late 12th century work. The church had probably attained its present size when it was dedicated to St Maelrubha in 1242 and was then one of the largest parish churches in Scotland. The nave is quite wide and has arcades of six bays on round piers opening into aisles, and there is a west tower with twin west lancets (very unusual) and a stair turret on the north side.   The tower has a short stone spire within a corbelled parapet and a tower arch with nook-shafts which was only re-opened in 1963. The church dedication had been changed to St Mary by 1517 when the Prioress of Haddington successfully applied for it to be made collegiate and the chancel then lengthened. However the chancel was later restored to about its original size and now has a 20th century vestry on the north side. The upper part of the north aisle wall was rebuilt in the 1790s and in 1815 the south aisle was rebuilt, a medieval south porch and various burial aisles being swept away along with the seating lofts of the Town Council, the Seamen and various other trades. Stones in the porch include a Celtic cross-slab with beasts and a tomb-slab of Sir James Ewart, college chaplain in 1544-55.

CREICH   Fife   *St Devenic*   NT 326214   8km NW of Cupar

This ruined church has a round-headed north lancet and a sharply pointed south door-way, perhaps both 14th century. There are two tomb recesses in the north wall with round arches with roll and hollow mouldings. The mutilated eastern recess had a keystone with the arms of the Barclays of Pearston, and once contained an incised slab of a knight and lady thought to be David Barclay, d1400 and his wife Helen Douglas, d1421 now removed the church of 1829-32 to the south. On the south side are low walls of an early 16th century transeptal aisle with the arch to it now blocked. The other openings are 18th century but on the rebuilt west gable is a stone with the date 1621.

Crichton Church

Cruggleton Church

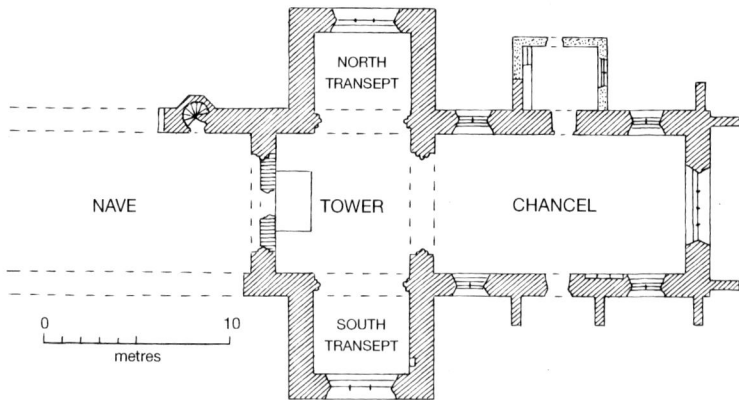

Plan of Crichton Church

CRICHTON Lothian *St Mary & St Kentigern* NT 381616 8km SE of Dalkeith

This cruciform church was built to serve a college founded by James II's chancellor Sir William Crichton in 1449. The low central tower extends west beyond the shallow transepts and has a saddleback roof recessed behind a parapet and plain mullioned windows. The south transept contains a piscina. The three bay chancel has two-light windows between buttresses on the south side, a four-light east window with modern tracery, and a modern porch on the site of a former vestry. Like the transepts the chancel has thick walls to support a plain tunnel-vault, and it contains a sacrament house and three sedilia. Below the eaves cornice is a second cornice. After the Reformation the wooden-roofed nave was destroyed except for a short section of the north wall with a projecting turret containing the staircase up to the tower, probably located where it is because of a screen beside it. The west arch of the tower was then blocked up with material including a small round-headed doorway and a panel with arms.

CRUGGLETON   Dumfries & Galloway   NX 478428   4km NW of Whithorn

Lying in a copse is an early 12th century nave and chancel church much restored c1890 at the expense of the 3rd Marquess of Bute. The chancel arch has two orders of shafts with bulbous bases, the inner order having reeded cushion capitals. The east window has an original round-arch head formed from a single slab. The chancel south wall appears to be all new. In the nave the west window, two windows on the south and the north and south doorways, the latter with nook-shafts with cushion-capitals, all represent original features but almost all of their stones have been renewed.

CULLEN   Aberdeenshire   *St Mary*   NJ 507664   1km SW of Cullen

This church existed in 1236 and was probably then a simple rectangle 18m long. In the 1320s Robert Bruce endowed a chantry priest here to pray for the soul of his late spouse Elizabeth de Burgh. In 1543 the church was made collegiate and the east end was lengthened (with a roof at a lower level) and the south transept added. The south and east windows are of that period, the latter with intersecting tracery and perhaps also the window-heads with Y-tracery in the south wall. The west window may be earlier but the other features and north transept and vestry are later. The south transept once contained an altar to St Anne. Here lies the grave-slab of John Duff, depicted in plate armour with the recut date 1404. The chancel contains a splendid sacrament house and an effigy of Alexander Ogilvie of Deskford, d1554.

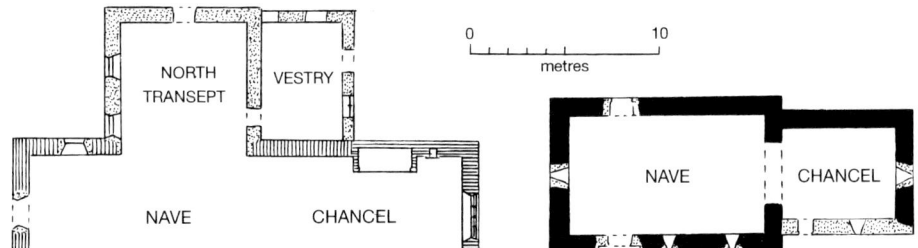

Plan of Cullen Church

Plan of Cruggleton Church

■ 13th Century

▨ 14th Century

▨ 15th Century

▤ 16th Century

▨ 17th Century

▨ Later & Modern

Cullen Church

CULROSS Fife *St Mungo* NS 990862 By the roadside east of the town

Excavations have exposed the lower parts of a chapel of St Mungo built c1500 by Robert Blackadder, Archbishop of Glasgow. Entered by a west doorway, it comprised a nave and an apsed chancel of equal width divided by a stone rood screen.

The West Kirk some way NW of the town at 980865 was the original parish church. No ancient openings survive but the lintels of the 17th century doorways are formed from medieval graveslabs incised with swords. The Bruce arms appear on the north gable of the crow-stepped burial aisle on the south side. The church was later abandoned in favour of the patched-up choir and transepts of the abbey church.

CUPAR Fife *St Michael* NO 373144 At south end of the town

In 1415 a new church with a tower at the NW corner of a fully aisled main body 40m long was begun in the town to replace an older church of St Christopher to the NW at 367153. By 1785 the new church was decayed and was demolished and rebuilt except for the tower and part of the north aisle converted into a session house. The two lowest levels of the tower are both vaulted. The top stage and the balustraded parapet around a spire with another balustrade halfway up were added in 1620. The 17th century monuments outside include a stone to three Covenanters executed in 1681.

DALGETY Fife *St Bridget* NT 169838 3km east of Inverkeithing

The blocked north doorway and most of the walling of the original single chamber go back to when the church was consecrated in 1244 by the Bishop of St Andrews. In the late 16th century galleries were inserted at either end (the outside stair of the east one still remains) and a transept called the Fordell Aisle was added on the north side. East of it lies the early 17th century burial vault of William Inglis of Otterston. The burial vault and laird's loft added at the west end c1610 by the Earl of Dunfermline is more like a small Z-plan tower-house, having a wing at the SW corner containing a retiring room with a fireplace and a polygonal staircase turret at the NE corner. The loft once had a plaster vaulted ceiling. The oldest memorial is that to William Abernethy, d1540.

Chancel doorway at Dalkeith

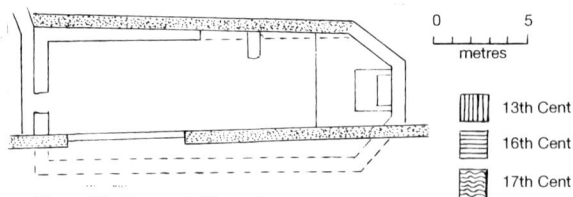

0   5
metres

13th Cent
16th Cent
17th Cent

*Plan of St Mungo's Chapel
at Culross*

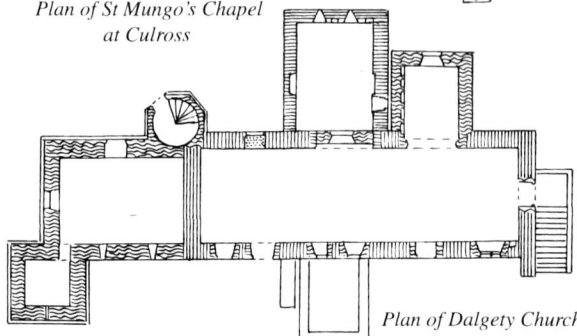

Plan of Dalgety Church

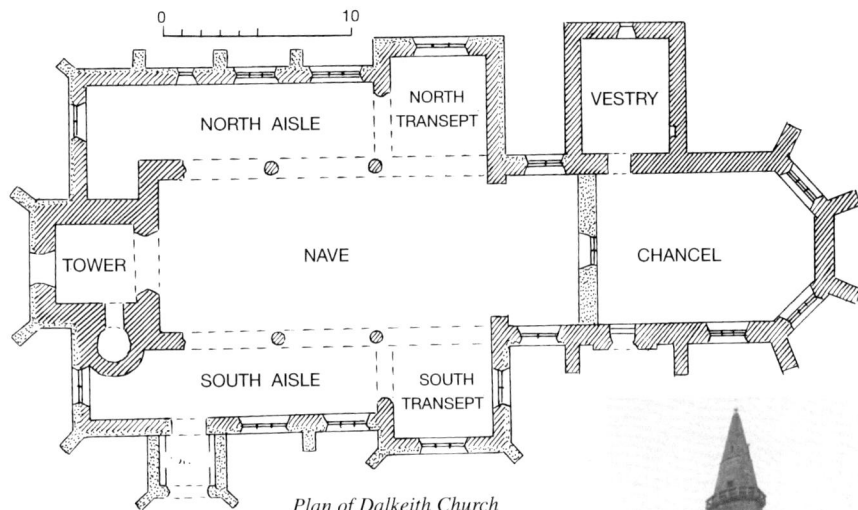

Plan of Dalkeith Church

Dalgety Church

Cupar Church

DALKEITH   Lothian   *St Nicholas*   NT 330670   At the NE end of the town

In 1372 Robert II licensed James Douglas to endow a chantry here and in 1390 James bequeathed money for repairs to what in 1406 became a collegiate chapel dependent on the church at Lasswade. The college had a provost and five prebendaries. The aisled nave with the eastern bay of the arcades opening into transepts must have existed by 1467, when the church obtained full parochial status. The short octagonal piers have moulded capitals and bell-bases. These parts remain in use and were refaced in 1851-4, when the west tower was rebuilt above its base and given a broach-spire. The porch perpetuates the old design, with a ribbed tunnel-vault. The chancel with loop tracery in its three-light windows, a fine but damaged south doorway, buttresses with image niches and an eaves cornice with foliage was built by James Douglas, 1st Earl of Morton c1480. It contains a tomb (page 14) with effigies of the earl in civilian dress and his wife Princess Joanna. Their feet rest on lions, his biting a skull and hers biting a dog. One of the earliest of the apsed chancels in Scottish parish churches, it was once covered by a ribbed tunnel vault which collapsed after this part (except for the west bay) was abandoned in 1590. On the north side is a vestry with two vaulted levels.

Dalmeny Church (see also page 6)

Sacrament house at Deskford

DALMENY   Lothian   *St Cuthbert*   NT 144775   2km SE of South Queensferry

Despite the original west tower being rebuilt in 1937 this is the finest and least altered 12th century parish church remaining in Scotland. Masons' marks suggest the same craftsmen also worked at Dunfermline Abbey and the church at Leuchars. The nave has a south doorway set in a projecting piece of wall with some blind intersecting arcading above. It has two orders of shafts and the signs of the Zodiac, an Agnus Dei and other figures appear on the arch., The nearly square chancel and the apse both have corbel tables, vaults with rolls and chevrons on the ribs, and are entered through good original arches with chevrons and triple shafts. The nave corbel table was destroyed when it was re-roofed in 1766. The tower arch with half-shafts is partly original and the restored windows on the south side approximate to the forms of the originals. All the windows rest on original stringcourses round the building. Near the south doorway but probably once on the north side of the chancel (i.e. the founder's tomb place) is a medieval coffin-lid with a beast at one end and Christ and the Apostles on the side. The long north transeptal Rosebery Aisle was added in 1671 but remodelled later.

DESKFORD   Aberdeenshire   *St John*   NJ 509617   5km south of Cullen

This ruin is notable for its sacrament house now preserved under a sheet of glass. It is inscribed "This Pnt Loveable Vark Of Sacrement Hous Maid To Ye Honour & Lovig Of God Be An Noble Man Alexander Ogilvy Of Yat Ilk & Elizabet Gordon His Spouse The Zier Of God 1551" Other old features are the ogival-headed piscina and stoup and the jambs of the SE doorway, all probably 16th century.

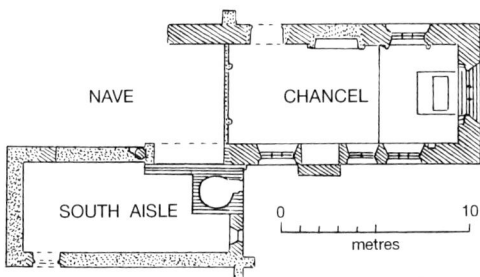

Plan of Douglas Church

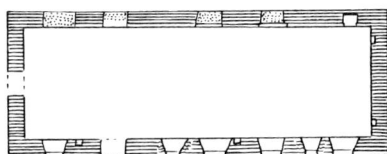

Plan of Deskford Church

12th Century
14th Century
16th Century
Later & Modern

Plan of Dalmeny Church

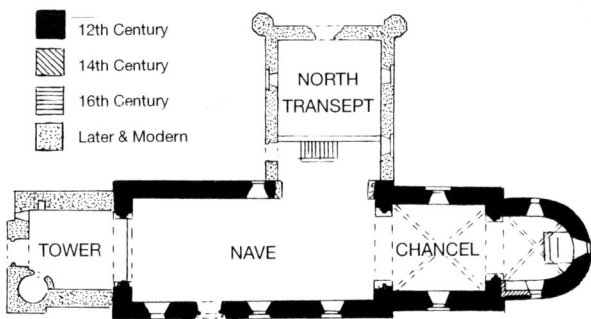

Douglas Church

Window at Dalmeny

DOUGLAS Lanarkshire *St Bride* NT 834310 At the north end of the village

In 1307 Sir James Douglas surprised and killed the English garrison of the nearby castle whilst they were attending a service in the church. It was probably in atonement for this act that Sir James, who died on crusade in 1330, built the present chancel, now the only part roofed. His cross-legged effigy lies in a recess in the north wall. An adjacent recess contains the effigy of Archibald, Earl of Douglas and Duke of Touraine, d1438, whilst in the south wall is a deep recess with effigies of James 7th Earl of Douglas, d1443 and his wife Beatrix Sinclair. There is also a tomb of Lady Elizabeth Douglas, Countess of Home. The church was abandoned for worship in 1780 and the aisle on the south side of the nave was mostly rebuilt in the 19th century to form a burial vault but the doorway is medieval and there remains an arcade of two blocked pointed arches. The recess in the eastern arch and the adjoining staircase-turret date from 1565, the year given on the turret clock. In the wall closing off the chancel are two 12th century capitals, probably from a former nave doorway.

Duddingston Church

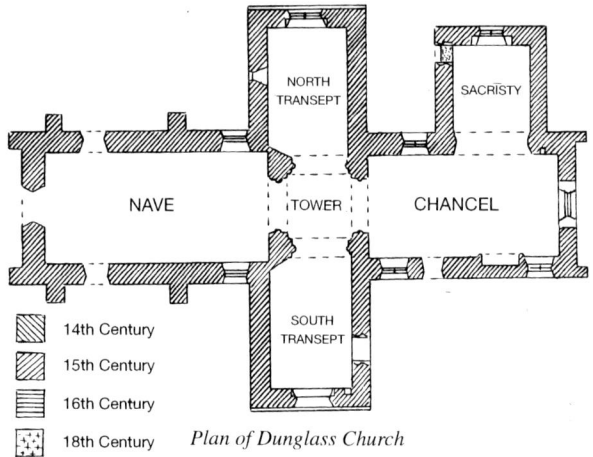

14th Century	
15th Century	
16th Century	
18th Century	

Plan of Dunglass Church

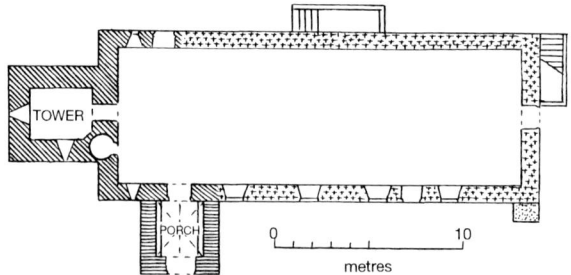

Plan of Duffus Church

DUDDINGSTON   Lothian   NT 284726   3km ESE of Edinburgh

The nave and chancel with pilaster buttresses are both 12th century. The blocked south doorway has chevrons on the voussoirs and herringbone and lozenge patterns on the jamb shafts. Also original are the chancel arch and chancel corbel table. The west tower with corner obelisks is 17th century and the Prestonfield Aisle on the north side is dated 1631 on the blocked doorway. The east and south windows and the heavy buttresses built against the pilasters are late 18th century and early 19th century.

DUFFUS   Moray   *St Peter*   NJ 173687   8km NW of Elgin

The main body of this ruin in state care is 18th century but the vaulted basement which is all that remains of the west tower is 14th century and the rib-vaulted south porch with a finely moulded outer arch is 16th century. South of the porch is the base of a medieval churchyard preaching cross.

DUMBARTON   Dunbartonshire   *St Mary*   NS 398756   Originally in middle of town

The tower arch which since 1907 has stood in College Park (394750) is the sole relic of a church mentioned in the early 14th century, now replaced by a railway station. The tower had a wooden spire and seems to have been added along with a new chancel and north transept after the church was made collegiate in 1450 with Isabella, Duchess of Albany and Countess of Lennox as patron. The building was derelict by 1758.

Sedilia in Dunglass Church

Interior of Duffus Church

Tower of St Mary's Church, Dundee

DUNDEE Angus *St Mary* NO 402302 City centre

This church was founded by David, Earl of Huntingdon before he became king in 1124. It was burned during English attacks on the town in 1296, 1385 and 1547 and was rebuilt in the 15th century as a large cruciform structure. Of the medieval building there remain only the large and lofty west tower with a west doorway of two round-arched openings under another round arch. Originally a porch, the tower basement later served as a prison. The tower was defended against General Monk in 1650, its garrison eventually being smoked out and massacred. By that time the church had been divided into three separate places of worship, St Clement's in the former nave rebuilt in the 18th century, St Paul's in the former transepts rebuilt in 1847, and the town church of St Mary in the former chancel rebuilt in 1844.

DUNGLASS Lothian *St Mary* NT 767718 12km SE of Dunbar

This cruciform building now in state care was built to serve a college founded by Sir Alexander Home in the 1440s. It has a low central tower narrower than any of the four arms, each of which retains a slab roof over a barrel-vault. Some of the windows are now just ragged holes and there is now a wide entrance where the east window used to be, a relic of a post-Reformation use of the building as a barn. Each transept has a tomb recess in the end wall, that on the north having the arms of the grandparents of Sir Alexander, i.e. Sir Thomas Home and his wife. The chancel retains segmental-headed windows with pairs of ogival-headed lights and three ogival-headed sedilia. On the north side a wide arch opens into a chapel or vestry. See page 13.

Dunning Church

Dysart Church

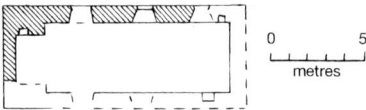

St Anthony's Chapel, Edinburgh

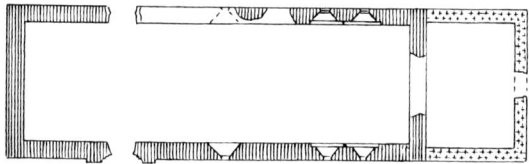

Plan of Dunstaffnage Chapel

DUNNING   Perth & Kinross   *St Serf*   NO 019145   14km SW of Perth

This church has a lofty late 12th century west tower with belfry windows of two lights set under a round arch and divided by renewed slender columns with cushion capitals. There is a staircase in the SW corner. The crow-stepped gables of the saddle-backed roof are later. There is a plain pointed arch to the nave which has some 12th century walling with a blocked doorway on the north side. Until rebuilding in 1810, when a transept was added, there was a lower and slightly narrower chancel of which the windowless north wall with its corbel-table remains. The east doorway is of 1687. In 2002 a fine 3m high cross originally erected in the 9th century on the hillside SW of Dupplin Castle was set under the tower. It bears scenes of King Constantine and the biblical King David, plus warriors and interlacing, the detailing being Pictish in style.

DUNSTAFFNAGE   Argyll   NM 881344   Near the shore 5km NE of Oban

The ruined chapel of c1225-50 lying in trees to the SW of the MacDougalls' castle is larger and finer than any parish church of its period in Argyll and is a monument in state care. There are roll mouldings on the corners and on the inner jambs of the twinned north lancets with round rere-arches and there are opposed north and south doorways. The east wall facing a Campbell burial enclosure of 1740 is reduced to its base.

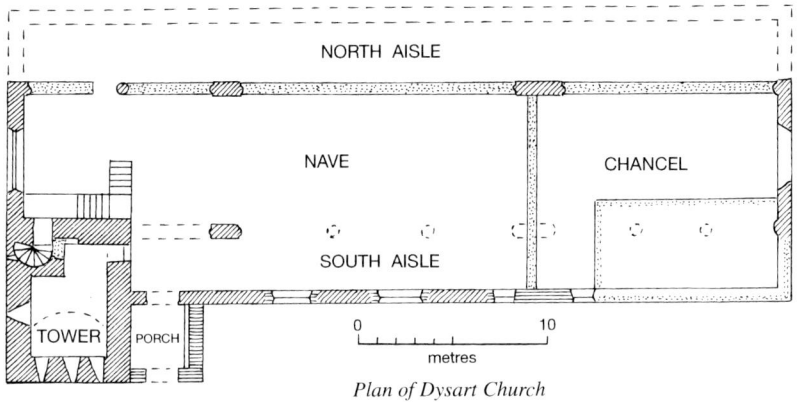

Plan of Dysart Church

DYSART Fife *St Serf* NT 303928 2km NE of Kirkcaldy

In 1802 the north aisle of the derelict fully aisled rectangle of eight bays built c1500 was demolished when a new road was made down to the harbour. It replaced a smaller church dedicated by Bishop David de Burnham in 1245. Some of the arcade piers remain but only the western ones still carry arches. The west bay on the south is filled by a rectangular six storey SW tower with a gabled roof set inside a plain corbelled parapet with a caphouse over the staircase in the NW corner. Beside is a later porch.

EDINBURGH Lothian *St Anthony* NT 276737 0.5km SE of Holyrood Palace

High on the north side of Arthur's Seat are remains of a small 14th century chapel built under royal patronage. The north wall still stands high with evidence of three bays of vaulting, a north doorway and domestic upper rooms in a higher west end.

Dunstaffnage Chapel

St Anthony's Chapel, Edinburgh

EDINBURGH   Lothian   *St Giles*   NT 257734   In the middle of the High Street

This was the only parish church in the burgh until the Reformation, hence its even-tual great size. It is first mentioned in 1178 but must have existed by the 1130s. The church seems to have had an aisled nave and a central tower and transepts when it was burned along with the town by Richard II of England in 1385. A contract survives for the building of five vaulted chapels beside the south aisle in 1387. These formed an outer aisle of which only the eastern part has survived later rebuilding, a porch and a second outer aisle of c1510-18 forming the chapel of the Holy Blood between the porch and the south transept having been swept away.

West of where a fine 12th century north doorway of three orders survived until 1796 is the two bay Albany aisle built by Robert, Duke of Albany and Archibald, 4th Earl of Douglas as part of a penance for their part in the murder of Robert, Duke of Rothesay at Falkland Palace in 1401. It bears their arms and has a vault boss with the monogram of the Virgin Mary. Only the east bay remains of the St John aisle of c1395 east of the former doorway. Four out of the five bays of the present fully aisled chancel together with the vestry east of the north transept were probably complete by 1419, when the town council applied to have the church made collegiate. A more successful applica-tion was made in 1467 after the chancel was lengthened and given a clerestory under patronage from James II's widow Mary of Gueldres. The south transept was length-ened and between it and the chancel south aisle the Preston aisle was begun in 1455 after Sir William Preston presented a holy relic in the form of an arm-bone of St Giles to the church. A boss on the chapel's tierceron vault like that of the chancel bears the arms of Patrick Hepburn, Lord Hailes and Provost of Edinburgh in 1487. A small chapel further south was added by Walter Chepman in 1507. The central tower was height-ened c1460-80 and c1500 was provided by the famous crown-spire.

St Giles, Edinbugh

In 1560 the medieval screens and furnishings were removed by Reformers. Dividing walls of c1581 allowing the building to be used by three separate congregations were removed during the periods when the church was used as a cathe-dral in 1633-8 and 1661-89, but only finally vanished in the restorations of the 1870s and 80s. In the early 19th century buildings encroaching on the outside walls were removed and by 1833 the whole of the exterior except for the tower and spire had been refaced and some parts remodelled. Vestries and other lower outer rooms were added in the 1880s and the Thistle chapel at the SE corner was added in 1909.

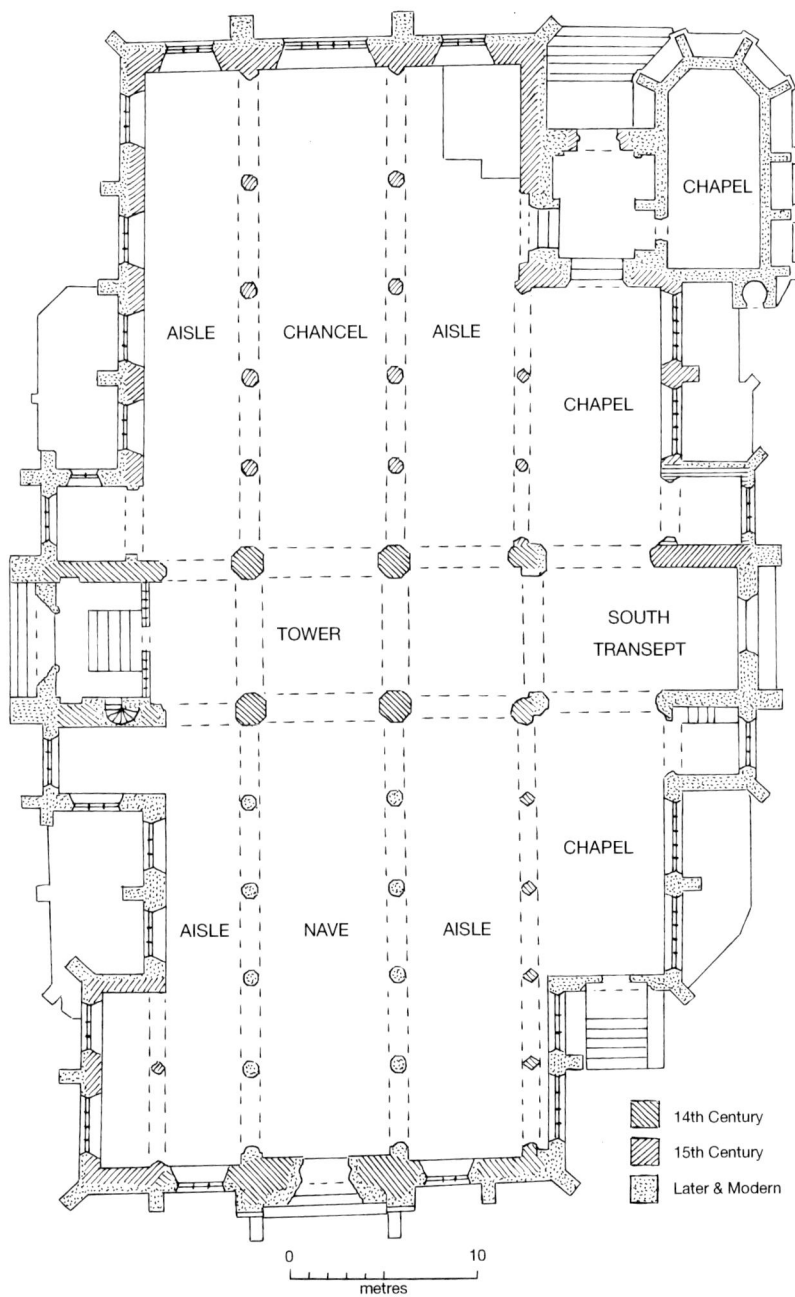

Plan of the church of St Giles at Edinburgh

EDINBURGH Lothian *Holy Trinity* NT 261737 North of High St in Old Town

James II's consort Mary of Gueldres founded a college of the Holy Trinity in Chalmers Close c1460. It had an aisled and apsed choir and transepts with a low saddleback roofed central tower, but the intended nave was never built. It served as a parish church from the 1580s until removed to make way for a railway in 1848. The stones were stored but many had been pilfered by 1872 when the choir alone without aisles was rebuilt on a new site between High Street and Jeffrey Street.

   In Cowgate is the much altered Magdalen Chapel of the 1540s with south windows and a north tower of the 1620s. It served a hospital founded by the MacQueen family and was later used as the convening hall of the Incorporation of Hammermen.

EDROM Borders *St Mary* NT 828558 5km NE of Duns

Thor Logos founded a church here c1105, but the good doorway with fine carvings now reset as the entrance to a burial vault is twenty or more years later. It has one order of shafts and arches with chevron and crenellation motifs. The south transept of the present church retains a pointed medieval arch and has on one of its diagonal buttresses an inscription recording repairs by Sir John Home of Blackadder in 1696. The main body must be somewhat earlier and the north aisle is of 1780 and 1886.

EGILSAY Orkney *St Magnus* HY 466304 On the west side of Isle of Egilsay

It is likely that the frequent visits here by Bishop William in 1135-8 were to oversee the construction of this church probably on the site of a smaller older building in which St Magnus prayed before he was killed in 1116. It consists of a tapering round west tower with tall slit windows in the outer faces and a nave and tunnel-vaulted chancel each with later crowstepped gables. The round-arched windows and doorways are mostly original but two rectangular windows in the south wall are probably 17th century. Over the chancel vault was a small upper room lighted by a tiny loop on the east gable.

Egilsay Church

Edrom: the reset chancel arch

ELGIN   Moray   *St Giles*   NJ 216629   In the middle of the High Street

A church of 1828 known as the Muckle Kirk stands on the site of the medieval parish church of Elgin which existed long before the cathedral came in the 1220s, and out-lived it. An old engraving made shortly before it was demolished shows a saddleback-roofed tower standing at the east end of an aisled nave three or four bays long without a clerestory. There was a window of four lancets over the west doorway, which was probably late 13th century, the likely date of the windows with Y-tracery at the west end of each aisle. Roof marks on the tower seem to have been the only relics of former transepts and a chancel removed sometime after the Reformation, perhaps as late as the rebuilding of 1684. By the 16th century the city guilds of the Hammermen, Glovers, Tailors, Shoemakers, and Weavers all had their own chapels within this church.

EUROPIE   Western Isles   *St Maelrubha*   NB 519652   Near NE corner of Lewis

This church of c1200 was restored in 1912 after being ruinous since the 1850s. The SW doorway and the single small window in each wall are round arched, but the east window has a pointed rere-arch. Recesses in the walls suggest the position of a screen and rood-beam. The end walls have wide plinths, that on the west returning for a short way along the south side. Of slightly later date are the tiny north vestry and south chapel, each with slit windows. The dedication to one of St Columba's mid 6th century companions suggests there was a much older church on the site.

EYE   Western Isles   NB 482322   By isthmus 6km east of Stornoway

In c1500 a chapel with round arched and rectangular windows, a round-arched south doorway and a western tomb recess was added to the west end of a wider 14th cen-tury main body with slit windows. The doorway east of the blocked original doorway may have led to a vestry or chapel. The doorway and high set window near the SW corner appear to be 17th century. Fixed on the south wall is a slab with a life-sized ef-figy of a knight of c1400. On the north wall is a slab carved with foliage and animals to Margaret MacLeod, d1503. A third medieval slab with a sword lies on the ground.

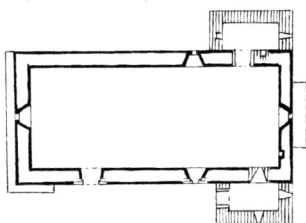

Plan of Europie Church

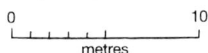

0   10
metres

Plan of Egilsay Church

Plan of Eye Church

Eye Church

Eynhallow Church

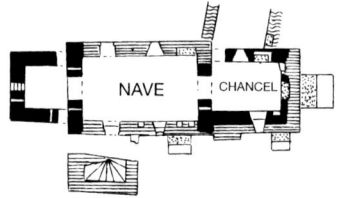

Plan of Eynhallow Church

0   10

metres

Plan of Fordyce Church

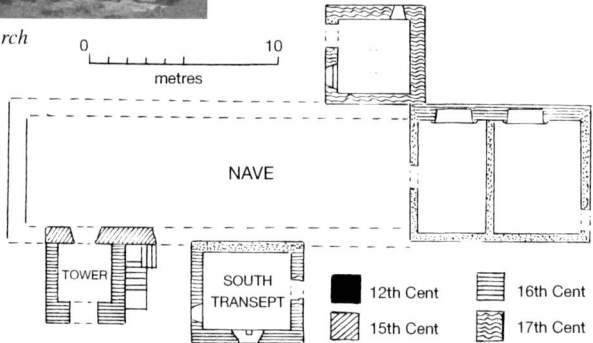

| ■ 12th Cent | ▤ 16th Cent |
| ▨ 15th Cent | ▩ 17th Cent |

Fordyce Church

Plan of Fowlis Easter Church

EYNHALLOW   Orkney   HY 359288   On island between Mainland and Rousay

A small church of c1200 comprising a nave and chancel with a pointed arch between them and a west porch perhaps intended to be carried up as a tower with a round arch to the nave was remodelled in the 16th century and later adapted for residential use with a staircase wing added on the south side. It ended up as three cottages which were unroofed when the island was cleared in 1851 but has been restored since.

FALKIRK   Falkirk   *St Modan*   NS 887800   On the south side of the town centre

The only parts of the aisled cruciform medieval church to remain are the 15th century crossing piers now supporting the northern corners of a tower of 1738 now lying on the south side of a main body of 1810. A church here is mentioned in the late 11th century. A mausoleum of 1810 of the earls of Zetland lies on the side of the medieval chancel and a porch-cum-session house of 1892 lies on the site of the south transept. The 18th century monument to Sir John Graham, killed in the nearby battle in 1298, includes a worn medieval effigy of a person in a robe. Inside the tower are worn effigies of a 15th century knight and lady and late 16th century effigies and other memorials to members of the family of Livingstone of Callander together with a roof boss with their arms.

FORDYCE   Aberdeenshire   *St Tarlarican*   SJ 554637   4km SW of Portsoy

Two burial enclosures incorporate part of the north wall of the chancel with early 16th century tomb recesses. The more elaborate of the two contains an effigy of one of the Ogilvie family. A 17th century burial vault adjoins this part. The only remaining part of the nave is a short section with the south doorway, in front of which is a 16th century porch continued up as a tower with a habitable upper room with a fireplace and a bellcote on top. Just east of this porch is a 16th century transeptal burial aisle with a panel with arms of the Abercromby family.

FORGANDENNY   Perth & Kinross   NN 088184   6km SW of Perth

The masonry of the main body is likely to be late medieval. The east wall of squared blocks is older and two 12th century windows are said to have been traced within it c1880. The south wall has a reset fragment of a 12th century arch adorned with chevrons. The existing windows are of 1902. The Ruthven Aisle on the south side is probably of c1600 but remodelled in the 1770s when the main body was heightened.

FOWLIS EASTER   Angus   *St Marnock*   NO 322335   10km west of Dundee

A church here is mentioned in 1180 but the present ashlar-faced structure was built in the 1450s by Andrew Grey. It has a fine four-light west window, a round-arched SW doorway and several other plain windows on the south side. The single window on the north side helped light the screen which divided the church. A loose doorway still survives from the loft over the screen. Other features of interest are the jougs by the doorway, the mutilated font, a sacrament house adorned with a scene of the Annunciation, and four late medieval paintings on oak depicting the Crucifixion, the Virgin, St John the Baptist and St Catherine. There is an old cross-slab lying outside.

Tomb at Fordyce   *Screen at Fowlis Easter*

Gamrie Church

GAMRIE Aberdeenshire *St John* NJ 791645 8km east of Macduff

The eastern end of this ruin picturesquely situated above the Moray Firth is thought to be the oldest part, although all of it seems to be quite late. The north wall is far from straight and has just one window where the screen must have been. The almost symmetrically arranged windows and doorways on the south side are 17th century, but such a long and narrow building was not ideal for Reformed forms of worship.

GRANDTULLY Perth & Kinross *St Mary* NN 886506 3km NE of Aberfeldy

The walls date from c1533 when Alexander Stewart endowed a curate and chaplain to say prayers for the souls of his family and James V. The small windows in the south wall are all blocked up and the north doorway appears to be 18th century, whilst the west end with windows either side of a south doorway seems to be a later extension to house a chaplain. Of greater interest is the wooden tunnel vault with a painted scheme of the 1630s imitating a panelled and coffered ceiling with monogrammed initials of Sir William Stewart, d1646 and his wife Dame Agnes Moncrieff, with the Four Evangelists and many coats of arms of various landed families.

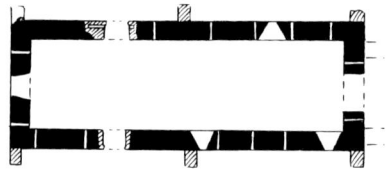

Haddington, St Martin: plan

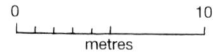

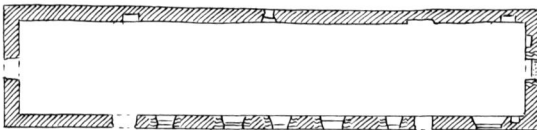

0   10
metres

■ 12th Century

▨ Later Medieval

▤ 16-17th Century

▦ Later & Modern

Plan of Gamrie Church

Grandtully Church

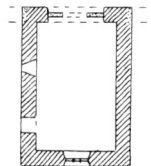

Guthrie: plan

Gullane Church

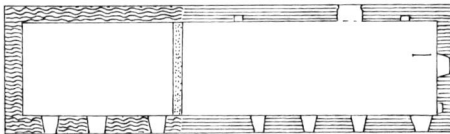

Plan of Grandtully Church

■ 12th Century

▨ 15th Century

▤ 16th Century

▧ 17th Century

▢ Later & Modern

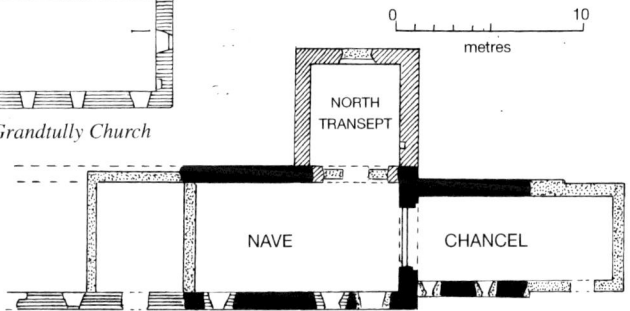

Plan of Gullane Church

GULLANE   Lothian   *St Andrew*   NT 483844   In village, 8km WSW of N. Berwick

In 1612 this church was abandoned in favour of a new church at Direleton because sand-dunes were encroaching on the churchyard. An arch with chevrons and nook-shafts with scallop capitals divides the 12th century nave and chancel. In the later medieval period the nave was given a north transept and was extended westwards.

GUTHRIE   Angus   *St Mary*   NO 567505   10km SSW of Brechin

This was an ancient foundation and was eventually made collegiate with a provost and four canons. The main body was replaced in 1826 but there survives the south transept dated 1479, now the Guthrie family burial place. It was added by Sir David Guthrie after he purchased the patronage from Arbroath Abbey and has a moulded mullioned south window and an old font. See photo on page 12,

HADDINGTON   Lothian   *St Martin*   NT 521740   East of the town

The surviving late 12th century nave was part of either the church of a Cistercian nunnery founded in 1178 by Ada de Warenne, or was possibly a chapel for layfolk set by the nunnery precinct gateway. The chancel arch with a hoodmould and plain imposts and the two south windows and one north window are all round-headed. The walls are pierced by a series of square holes of uncertain purpose. The doorways and buttresses are additions of a later period when a pointed vault was added. See page 11.

HADDINGTON   Lothian   *St Mary*   NT 519735   At SE bcorner of the town

The existing church here recorded as under construction in the 1460s is one of the largest of its type, still standing complete in a spacious open graveyard. It is a fully aisled building 63m long with a four bay chancel, a five bay nave and a low central tower with transepts. The priests serving the many altars were organised as a college c1540. Just eight years later the wooden roof of the nave and the stone vaults of the other parts were destroyed during a siege of the town by the English. The nave was later repaired for worship in the Reformed manner but the other parts remained roof-less until restoration in the 1970s. They were then given fibreglass vaults and the miss-ing NW corner of the north transept was rebuilt. The plaster vault over the nave and the upper parts of the aisle walls and buttress pinnacles formed part of a restoration in 1811 by James Burn. He also raised the nave arcades, which were once like those in the choir. The medieval north vestry was converted into the Lauderdale Museum in 1595 and contains a marble monument to John Maitland, Lord Thirlestane, d1595, his wife Jane Fleming and their son John, 1st Earl of Lauderdale and his wife Isabella Se-ton, who both died in 1638. This part has an east window of 1877, whilst the choir has several 20th century windows. In 1682 Agnes Black erected a tabernacle in the south transept to her husband William Seton, Provost of Haddington. See page 10.

HAMILTON   Lanarkshire   NS 727560   NE of the town centre

An 18th century print shows the apsed late medieval choir still roofed but with no west wall, and with a round arch leading through to a north transept, also still roofed. There were three-light windows in the apse and a row of lancets along the south side, below one of which was a 17th century square-headed doorway. The church lay just east of the former palace and the last traces of it have gone since the 1930s, the monument of the 3rd Duke of Hamilton having been transferred to the church at Bothwell.

Hamilton Church

West doorway of St Mary's Church at Haddington

VESTRY

CHANCEL

NORTH TRANSEPT

TOWER

SOUTH TRANSEPT

AISLE

NAVE

AISLE

0   10

metres

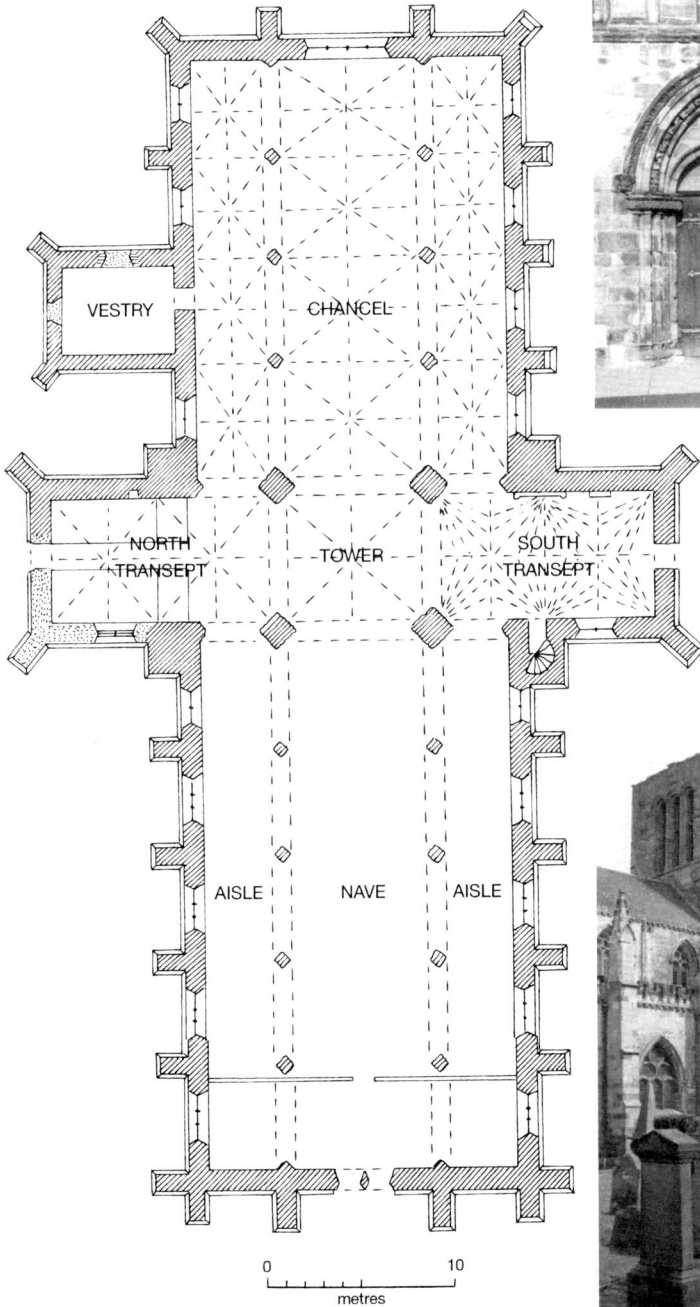

Haddington, plan of St Mary's Church

Haddington: St Mary's Church

Tower at Inverness

Tower at Inverkeithing

INVERNESS   Highland   *St Mary*

NH 666454   North of city centre

At the west end of the Old High Church of 1769-72 with porches and south apse of 1891 stands a lofty 16th century tower. It has one external offset and ends in a bal-ustraded parapet probably of 1649 around an octagonal belfry capped by a spire.

HIRSEL   Borders   NT 830406   1km NW of Coldstream

Excavations have shown that a small 10th century nave was later given an apse. It was lengthened to the west and given a thick end wall to support a bell turret in the 13th century. Later abandoned, the nave was used as a residence and then as a barn until burnt down, probably during an early 16th century English raid or invasion.

INVERKEITHING   Fife   *St Peter*   NT 130830

On east side of main street

The main body of the church was rebuilt after a fire 1825, leaving only the good 14th century west tower and the splendid font of c1398. The tower has a polygonal stair turret at the SE corner, buttresses at the other corners, two-light belfry windows and a low 16th century parapet on corbels surrounding a lead-covered spire of 1835 which replaces another put up in 1731. The font has a six-sided bowl on clustered shafts. Each side has an heraldic panel held by an angel. Apart from the royal arms and those of Robert III and Annabella Drummond there are arms of the families of Stewart, Foulis of Colinton with Bruce of Balcaskie, Melville of Glenbervie, and Ramsay of Denoune.

Font at Inverkeithing

St Oran's Chapel, Iona

Innerpeffray Church

St Oran's, Iona: plan

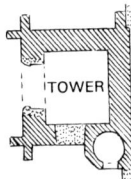

TOWER

Inverkeithing

0   5
metres

■ 12th Century	▨ 14th Century	☰ 16th Century	
□ c1200	▨ 15th Century	▨ Later & Modern	

St Ronan's, Iona: plan

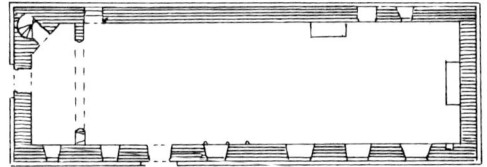

Plan of Innerpeffray Church

INNERPEFFRAY   Perth & Kinross   *St Mary*   NN 902184   5km SE of Crieff

This long, low building with a plinth all round it was built as a collegiate church by Lord Drummond in 1508, but it stands on the site of a chapel mentioned in 1342. The doorway and squint on the north side mark the site of a destroyed vestry. The western end has a room above with a fireplace in the end gable. It is reached by a spiral stair in the NW corner. Three corbels on the inner side of the south wall are likely to be relics of a former screen and rood-loft removed at the Reformation. All the windows lie on that side and are square-headed, although the doorway has a pointed head.

IONA   Argyll   *St Ronan*   NM 285241   On island at the west end of Mull

In the precinct of the nunnery is the ruined former parish church of St Ronan dating from c1200, although the first mention of it is in 1372. Excavations showed the church replaced an earlier chapel with clay-bonded walls, part of an altar table being found. The church has a round-headed east window and restored windows near the east end of the north and south walls. The west end has been rebuilt. The church was given a glass roof in 1923 to protect a collection of carved stones. Close to the abbey is the 12th century chapel of St Oran which was the burial place of the MacDonald Lords of the Isles. It has a narrow window towards the east end of the north and south walls, an original west doorway, a 15th century tomb recess in the south wall, and a blank east wall. Only fragments of the north and south walls now remain of a chapel of St Mary.

KEIL Argyll *St Columba* NR 673077 Near Southend, end of Kintyre Peninsular

This long and rather overgrown ruin has a 13th century eastern part with two south windows and one north window, but the twin east lancets have been lost, whilst the west end with its round-arched window is 16th century. The church was abandoned by the late 17th century. Amongst the tapered slabs dating from the 14th century to the early 16th century is one with a military effigy with a galley and a stag and hounds.

KEILLS Argyll *St Cormaic* NR 691805 18km SW of Lochgilphead

This small 12th century chapel has a round-headed window and two aumbries in the east wall, and an original window on each side. Two other south windows, one with a flat-lintelled rere-arch, are later. The church was abandoned in the late 17th century but in 1978 was re-roofed to protect a surperb 8th or 9th century cross brought in from the hillside above and a collection of over forty carved stones ranging from Early Christian slabs with crosses and plaits to tapered slabs of the 13th through to the 16th century. One of the slabs has a good image of a clarsach as well as six other varied motifs.

KILCONQUHAR Fife *St Columba* NO 485020 Near loch, 2km north of Elie

The three bay late medieval arcade for a former south aisle is incorporated into a burial enclosure. The corbel at the east end may be for a rood beam. A 16th century slab incised with a scull and crossbones lies south of the new church of 1819-21 nearby.

East windows at Kilmory

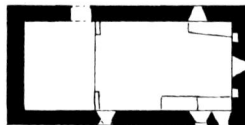
Keills: plan

Kilmory: plan

Arcade at Kilconquhar

Effigies at Kilmory

KILLEAN Argyll *St John* NR 695445 On west side of Kintyre opposite Gigha

This church abandoned in 1770 has lost its west wall. It has a 12th century nave with two windows on each side and a chancel of c1220 with moulded corners, roll mouldings around the two east windows with dogtooth ornamentation. and two other windows and a blocked priest's doorway. The nave doorway is later medieval. On the north side is the Largie family vault, perhaps 16th century, with a pointed vault and round-headed windows.

KILMORY Argyll *St Mary* NR 702751 W side of Knapdale,18km NW of Tarbert

The finely moulded south doorway and the segmental rere-arch of an adjacent south window date the chapel to the early 13th century, despite it having two small round-arched windows . The chapel was re-roofed in 1934 below wall-head height to protect a fine collection of over thirty stones, from Early Christian ones with ringed crosses to 14th to 16th century tapered slabs with a variety of motifs plus military and priestly effigies. There is also a 3m high cross with Christ crucified with St Mary and St John and an inscription referring to Alexander MacMillan keeper of Castle Sween in the 1470s.

KILMUN Argyll *St Munn* NM 166820 5.5km north of Dunoon

All that survives of a collegiate church begun on an older site in 1442 by Sir Duncan Campbell of Lochawe are a ruined west tower and a tomb with effigies of Duncan and his second wife Margaret. The tomb lies between the mausoleum of 1795 of the Dukes of Argyll on the site of the former vestry and the former choir. In 1688 the latter was renovated for parochial use and repaired in 1792, but replaced by a new T-plan church of 1841. The tower has three storeys connected by a spiral staircase in the SW corner. There was also an attic within the parapet. The upper room with a fireplace must have formed a residence for a priest. A few 14th to 16th century tapered slabs also remain.

Plan of Keil Church

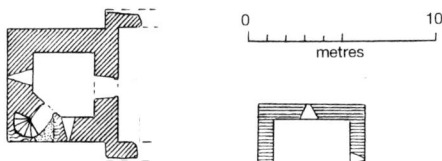

0   10

metres

Kilmun: plan

Plan of Killean Church

Tower at Kilmun

Kincardine Church

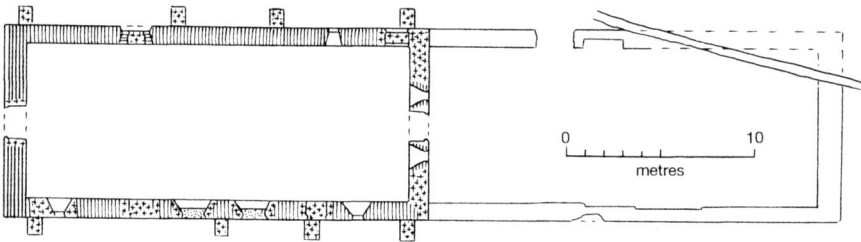
Plan of Kincardine Church

KILRENNY Fife *St John* NO 575049 In Kilrenny, 1km NE of Anstruther Easter

The 15th century tower with a pair of lancets on each side and a spire and corbelled parapet of the 16th century now lies NW of a church of 1807. The medieval nave east of the tower is known to have had an aisle on each side.

KINCARDINE Aberdeen *St Erchard & St Mary* NO 594994 7km ENE of Aboyne

This wide 13th century church served a hospital founded by Alan Durward. Foundations east of the 18th century east wall, in which are reset two lancets, indicate a building once over 42m long internally, although half of it seems to have served as an infirmary hall. The surviving part has blocked original north doorway and a lancet in each of the north and south walls. The symmetrical arrangement of windows and doorways (all now blocked) on the south side date from an 18th century remodelling. See p6.

KINGHORN Fife *St James* NT 273870 On headland to the east of the town

To the east of the wide church of 1774 on the site of the medieval nave are fragments of the north and east walls of the old chancel with evidence of two windows on the north and a chapel on the south. Bishop Burnham dedicated the church in 1243.

KINKELL   Aberdeenshire   *St Michael*   NJ 785191   3km SSE of Inverurie

This church fell out of use in the 18th century and is now much ruined but it retains the north jamb of a large 16th century east window, an incised slab depicting Gilbert de Greenlaw, who was killed at the battle of Harlaw in 1411, and a good sacrament house near the NE corner dated 1524 with initials of Rector Alexander Galloway.

KINNEIL   Falkirk   NS 982806   2km SW of Bowness

Only the west wall still stands of this 12th century church which was held by Holyrood Abbey. The double bellcote is later. In 1951 footings of the short nave and chancel divided by a narrow arch were laid bare. Under one of the walls of the aisle later added on the south side was found a cross now in one of the cellars of the nearby house. Probably 11th or 12th century, it has a hand of God above the head of a stiffly out-stretched Christ and was probably perched above the chancel arch facing the nave.

KIRKCALDY   Fife   *St Brycedale*   NT 280917   Off Kirk Wynd In middle of town

At the west end of the main body of 1806-8 (repaired in 1987 after a fire) is an ashlar-faced tower of c1500 with a stringcourse under the bell-chamber with a lancet on each sidr and a plain corbelled parapet around a small belfry of c1750.

Kinneil Church

Sacrament house at Kinkell

Tower of Kirkcaldy Church

c1200

15th Century

16th Century

16th Century

Later & Modern

NORTH TRANSEPT

VESTRY

TOWER

NAVE

0   10

metres

Kirkliston Church

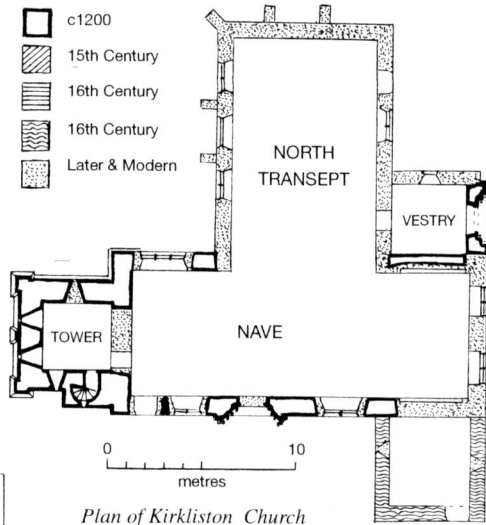

Plan of Kirkliston Church

KIRKLISTON   Lothian   NT 126744   In village, 4km south of Forth Road Bridge

Of c1190-1210 are the nave with a fine south doorway of four orders with chevrons and crocket capitals and the west tower with clasping buttresses, tiny lancets, a battered plinth and a stair-turret on the south side. The saddleback roof on the cut-down third storey of the tower is later. When a large north transept was added in 1883 the nave north doorway was reset in the east wall of a vestry tucked into the NE corner. The original nave windows were set above a string course which the present windows all cut into. A vault and loft of 1629 of the earls of Stair adjoins the SE corner.

LADYKIRK   Ayrshire   *St Mary*   NS 386267   4km east of Prestwick

A track now runs across the site of the nave. In trees on the south side is a small rectangular late medieval tower with a circular stair-turret. A corbelled parapet surrounds a top stage covered by a short stone spire. One window has a cusped head.

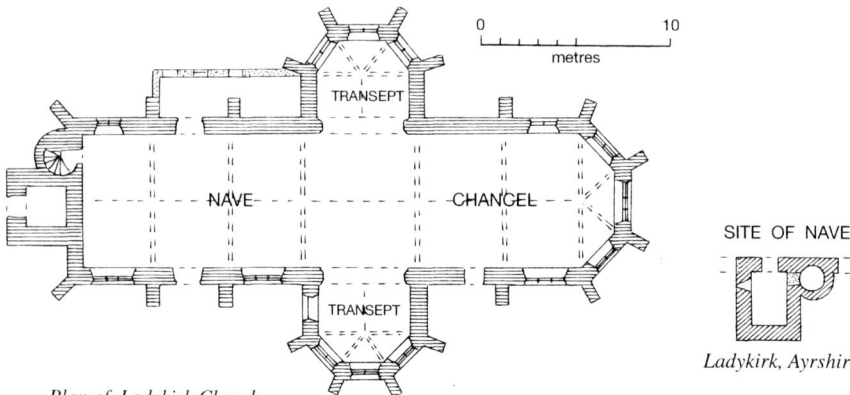

0   10

metres

TRANSEPT

NAVE   CHANCEL

TRANSEPT

SITE OF NAVE

Plan of Ladykirk Church

Ladykirk, Ayrshire

Ladykirk Church

LADYKIRK   Borders   *St Mary*   NT 889477   On the north side of the village

This collegiate church also known as the Kirk of Steill was built under patronage by James IV and replace a more modest building that had served Easter Upsettlington since at least the 13th century. A mention of glazing in 1507 suggests that the church was then nearly complete, although it was not until the 1740s that the small west tower was finished, being given its topmost storey to a design by William Adam. The lowest level does not communicate with the church and the room above reached by a stair-case in a circular NE turret seems to have been habitable. The church is remarkable for having stone-flagged roofs over barrel-vaults throughout and also for having not only an east apse but a pair of apsed transepts as well. There the vaults have radial ribs and the roofs end on gables over the transept arches rather than joining the main roof. The main vault has widely spaced cross-ribs. Bold buttresses with set-offs half way up and small pinnacles help to carry the vaults. There are three-light windows in the nave and chancel south walls and in the east bay of the main apse. The other windows are of two lights with Y-tracery. There are opposed north and south doorways in the nave, a priest's doorway in the chancel and a fourth doorway in the south transept west wall. From the 1790s until the 1860s the nave was closed off for use as a school.

LAMINGTON   Lanarkshire   *St Ninian*
NS 978309   9km SW of Biggar

A blocked doorway of c1190 with roll-moulded arches with chevrons and other motifs and formerly with one or-der of rather short shafts remains on the north side of a church otherwise rebuilt above the foundations in 1707 band remodelled in the 19th century.

Doorway at Lamington

Lanark Old Church

LANARK Lanarkshire *St Kentigern* NS 888432 At SE end of the town

This church was abandoned in favour of a new building in 1777. The early 13th century nave has five lancets and a doorway on the south side, a west doorway and a chancel arch set oddly off centre so that there is space for an east facing lancet beside it. The north arcade of six pointed double-chamfered arches on circular piers reconstructed in 1954 is probably of later in the 13th century. The aisle was eventually wider than the nave and its north doorway was discovered in a 19th century excavation.

Leuchars Church

LASSWADE Lothian *St Edwin* NT 302661

9km SE of Edinburgh

A three-stage west tower of c1200 with high east and west gables collapsed whilst under repair in 1866 and has now vanished. Also then surviving was a section of the nave south wall with a round-arched doorway. A 15th century high relief military effigy survives amongst the three burial aisles formerly attached to the north wall.

LEGERWOOD Borders NT 594434

7.5km SE of Lauder

The 12th century chancel has small original north and south windows and a chancel arch with shafts on either side of each respond. There are cushion capitals, and also scallops and volutes on the north side. Corner shafts suggest the chancel was intended to be vaulted. This part was walled off as the Kerr vault until 1898 and contains a monument to John Ker Morristoun and his wife Grizell Cochrane, d1748. The nave is also mostly 12th century but with a north transept and windows of the 19th century.

0   10
metres

■ 12th Century
▦ 13th Century
▨ 17th Century
▦ Later & Modern

NORTH AISLE

NAVE

Plan of Lanark Old Church

NORTH TRANSEPT

NAVE   CHANCEL

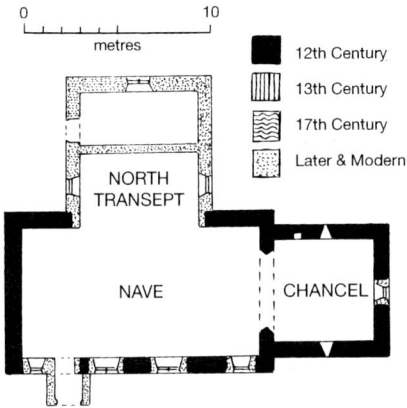

Plan of Legerwood Church

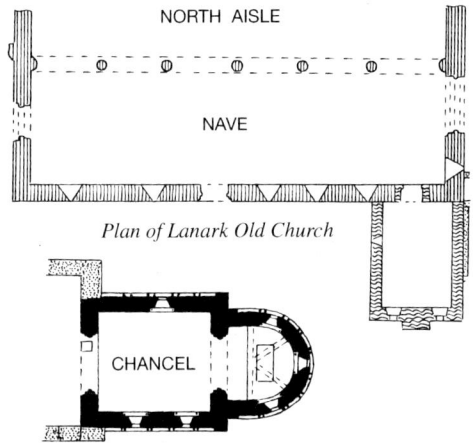

CHANCEL

Leuchars: plan

LEUCHARS   Fife   *St Athernase*   NO 455214   On rising ground north of village

The nave was lowered in height in 1745 and then totally rebuilt wider than before in 1857, but the mid 12th century square chancel and lower apse still survive, both having two tiers of external blind arcading separated by a string-course and corbel-tables with animal and human faces. The arches are carved with billets, chevrons and pearl-like motifs and intersect in the lower section on the chancel. There are cushion capitals on the piers, which are in pairs on the lower tier. Some of the arcading was restored in 1857. The octagonal belfry and lantern on the apse date from c1700.

Leuchars Church

LINCLUDEN   Dumfriess & Galloway   NX 967779   2km NW of Dumfries

This was originally the site of a Benedictine nunnery and once had a 12th century nave with a west doorway adorned with chevrons and north and south aisles of four bays, the SE respond still remaining, although the other parts were rebuilt later. In 1389 Archibald, 3rd Earl of Douglas got the nunnery suppressed so that the buildings could be taken over by a college consisting of a provost, eight prebendaries or secular canons and 24 bedesmen. A fine recess in the north wall of the choir contains a tomb of Robert III's daughter Margaret, d1450, widow of the 4th Earl of Douglas, (the effigy may not be of her). The choir was evidently begun in the 1440s to contain it and provide space for more prebendaries, one of them endowed by Margaret herself and others by the Douglas and Maxwell families. It was probably designed by John Morow from Paris, who also worked at the abbeys of Melrose and Paisley. A south aisle and south transept were also added about that time. The fall of the Douglases in 1455 probably caused a pause in the work, which has heraldry indicating completion c1500. The college buildings passed into secular hands and were made into a mansion held by the Maxwells. The church was partly re-roofed in 1629 but was abandoned by 1700.

The surviving parts of the church are all of sandstone ashlar blocks with a splayed plinth and a string-course below the windows. The whole building was originally covered with rib-vaults and there was also a vaulted crypt entered from the south side below the east end. The eastern bay of the south arcade corresponded to a transept with diagonal corner buttresses and a four-light south window. Only traces remain of complex tracery in the two remaining bays of the south aisle. All that remains of the nave north wall are footings with a tomb recess in the north-east corner.

The western parts of Lincluden Church

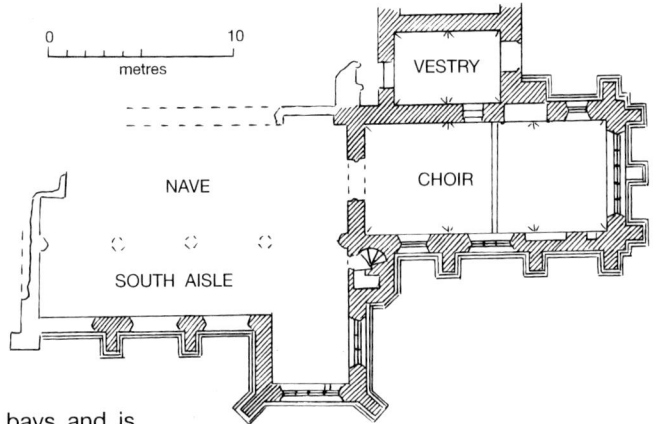

Plan of Lincluden Church

The choir is of three bays and is entered from the nave through a pulpitum screen with a basket-arch with the west face of the arch sill carved with cherubs, angels and scenes from the life of Christ. The choir has set-back corner buttresses at the east end, where there is a five-light window. On the south side are a piscina and sedilia and on the north side are the tomb recess and an equally elaborate doorway with nook-shafts leading through to a vestry which is one of a series of vaulted rooms in a two storey range extending northwards. Two south windows were of three lights but the western bay had a window of just two lights with a circle above because it was squeezed against a staircase turret in the angle with the transept. Most of the arms on the label stops of the hoodmoulds of the windows relates to the Douglases, but the Haliburton arms appear on the SW window and the Herries arms on the NE window.

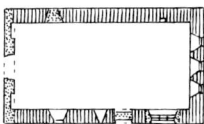

Logie: plan (see page 68)

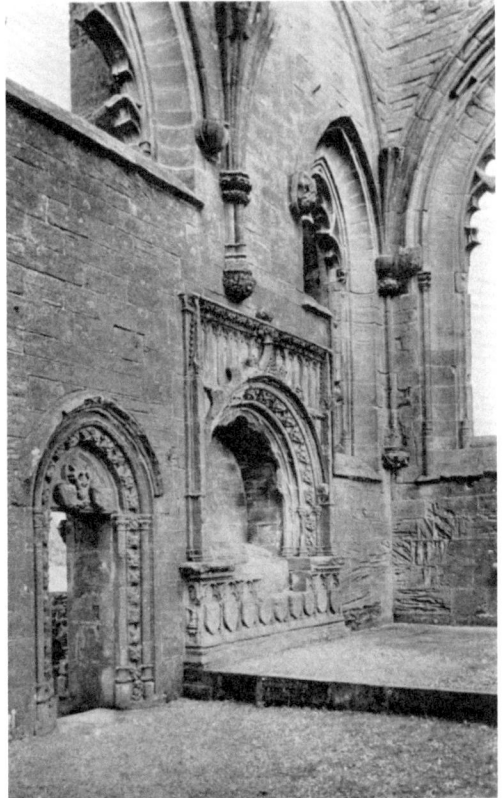

The choir of Lincluden Church

LINLITHGOW   Lothian   *St Michael*   NT 002773   By palace in middle of the town

The church lies just to the SE of the ruined royal palace on a promontory above a loch. The five bay nave of c1440-50 replacing an older church burnt in 1424 and the three bay chancel and east apse of c1500-35 together measure 54m long. There are transeptal chapels opening off the nave eastern bay. The church was divided into two by blocking the chancel arch in the restoration of 1812 but in 1894-6 it was opened out again, the galleries removed, and a new vestry built on the site of the medieval one. The two storey porch has an oriel and a crow-stepped roof the same height as that on the south transeptal chapel. The chancel windows have loop-tracery. The south chapel window is a fine specimen with a curved transom which forms with the window head a convex equilateral triangle within which three circles alternate with large dagger forms, all subdivided. The arcades are high and there are stone vaults over the aisles but only a shallow profiled plaster vault over the main span. The west tower has a polygonal NW staircase turret and corner pinnacles on the embattled parapet. The aluminium spire of 1964 is a reminder of the original crown-spire taken down c1820 because it was insecure. In the south aisle of the chancel is a slab to John Forest, Provost of Linlithgow, d1589. In the vestry are two relief slabs from a rare 15th century Passion retable showing the Agony in the Garden, the Betrayal, and the Mocking of Christ. The town also had a chapel of St Mary of c1490 standing by almshouses at the East Port.

LINTON   Borders   NT 774263   9km SE of Kelso

Both the nave and chancel have 12th century walling although both seem to have been shortened in the 18th century. A very fine tympanum of that period probably by a Herefordshire sculptor and depicting St George and the Dragon has been reset in the outer arch of the porch added when the south side was rebuilt in 1858. There are also two animal heads from a corbel-table. A vestry may have been added in the 1420s.

LOGIE   Angus   *St Martin*   NO 706635   6km north of Montrose

The 13th century chancel has triple east lancets with the middle one wider and higher. The SW window and the aumbry of a sacrament house near the NW corner are later medieval. The south doorway looks old but may have been moved. The west wall and doorway dates from 1857, when the chancel became a Carnegie family burial place.

Linlithgow Church   see also page 11

Logie Church

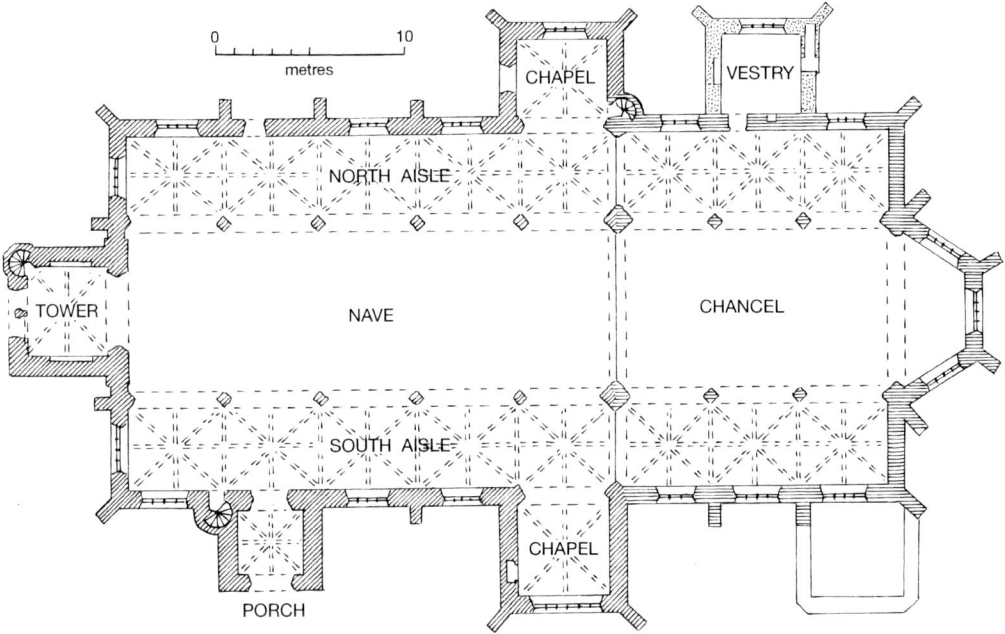

Plan of Linlithgow Church

South side of Linlithgow Church

Maybole Church

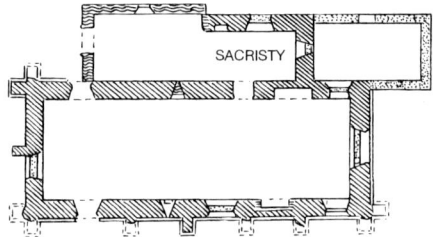

SACRISTY

Midcalder Church

Plan of Maybole Church

MARKINCH   Fife   *St Drostan*   NO 298020   At N end of village, E of Glenrothes

The main body of the church is of 1786 with alterations of 1884-5 and a north aisle of 1806, but there is a lofty ashlar-faced west tower of c1200 with two-light belfry openings with cushion capitals on the central and angle shafts and stringcourses between the four stages. The existing spire is of 1807 but replaces an older one. See page 7.

MAYBOLE   Ayrshire   *St Mary*   NS 300094   E side of town, 12km SSW of Ayr

This collegiate church was built in the 1370s by John Kennedy of Dunure. It is of rough rubble but once had features of some distinction. The south side was a show front of five bays divided by buttresses now mainly torn away. There is a shield over the doorway in the west bay which has three moulded orders with dogtooth ornamentation on the outermost. There are remains of a pair of two-light windows and a narrower window with a piscina in its embrasure. The three-light east window with reticulated tracery and the west window are now blocked and the tomb recesses on either side lie empty. On the north side is a small sacristy beside which is a 17th century extension which extends far enough west to partly block the main north doorway.

METHVEN   Perthshire   *St Marnoch*   NO 025260   In village, 9km WNW of Perth

The church was consecrated in 1247. It was made collegiate by Walter Stewart, Earl of Atholl in 1433 and remained in use until replaced by the adjacent present church of 1783. The college had a provost, five chaplains and four choirboys. Extra prebends were added c1510-15 and the surviving north transept was one of two probably added then. It has a blocked three-light window with reticulated tracery under a crowstepped gable and flanked by an image niche and a panel of the Royal Arms of James IV.

MIDCALDER   Lothian   NT 074673   In village, 3km east of Livingston

A thick wall carrying a Victorian belfry divides the choir from a transept of 1863. In 1542 Sir John Sandilands agreed to complete the choir and erect a nave, steeple and porch within three years, although there is no evidence these other parts ever existed. The choir has two wide bays and an apse with a lower rectangular vestry beyond to the east, under which is the Sandilands family burial vault. The corbels on the north side of the choir were for the roof of the southern walk of a intended cloister which is mentioned in the 1542 deed. Clearly the church was intended to be collegiate. There is a tomb recess internally on this side. On the south side is a round-arched doorway and a four-light window with loop tracery. The apse also has a four-light SE window.

MORTLACH   Moray   *St Moluag*   NJ 324393   At south end of Dufftown

The harled main body of the church is at least partly of c1200 as it has a round-headed north doorway with a drawbar-slot, two small east lancets and another lancet facing south at that end. By the NE corner is a recess containing a military effigy of Alexander Leslie, d1549. The other features are 19th century, when the transept was added.

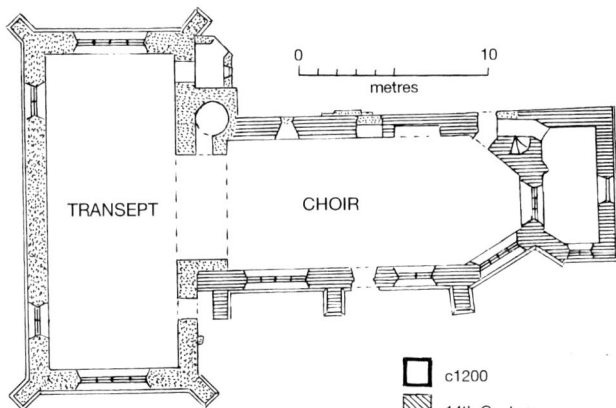

0   10
metres

TRANSEPT | CHOIR

☐ c1200
▨ 14th Century
▤ 16th Century
▧ 17th Century
▦ Later

Plan of Midcalder Church

Transept at Methven

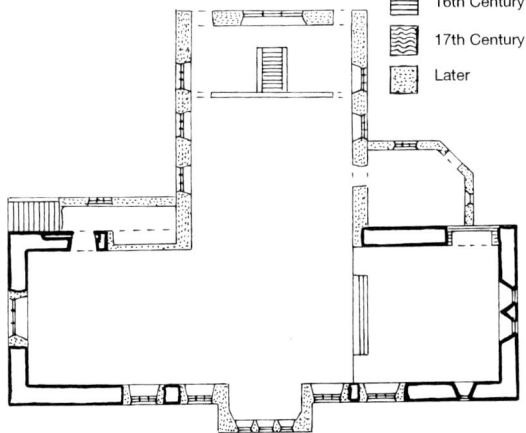

Plan of Mortlach Church

Mortlach Church

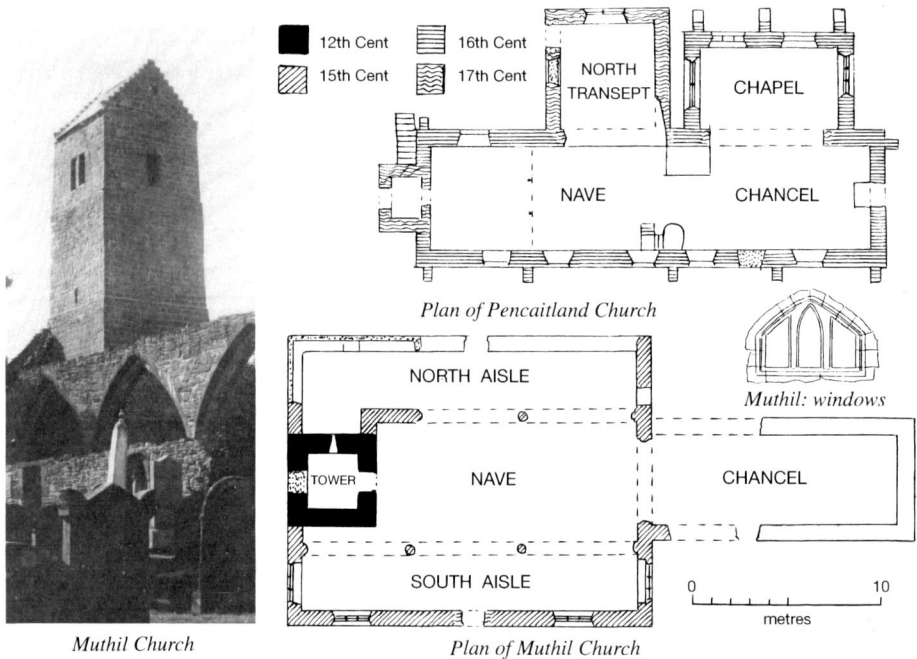
Muthil Church

■	12th Cent	▤	16th Cent
▨	15th Cent	▧	17th Cent

Plan of Pencaitland Church

Muthil: windows

Plan of Muthil Church

MUTHIL   Perth & Kinross   NN 869170   5km south of Crieff

The high saddleback-roofed 12th century tower now lies within the western end of the aisled nave built in the 1420s by Michael Ochiltree, Dean of Dunblane. The belfry windows facing west and north have each have a pair of round-arched lights with an octagonal pier with a cushion-capital and tapering semi-circular responds. The southern window is 17th or 18th century. The lower stages have tiny loops. The north arcade joined to the tower has two bays, whilst the south arcade carries on past the tower for a full three bays. The arches are simply moulded and spring directly from octagonal piers, the chancel arch being similar. The outer walls are reduced on the north side and only footings remain of the chancel, which was demolished after the Reformation. The north aisle has an east doorway which led to a sacristy beside the chancel. The south aisle has original low three-light windows facing east, south and west. The doorway is 17th century. Under the tower now lies a single stone bearing two worn effigies said to be of Sir Muriel Drummond of Concraig, d1362, and his wife Ada. See page 5.

NEWLANDS   Borders   NT 161465   5km south of W. Linton, 16km SW of Penicuik

The set-back west gable and round-arched SW doorway may be of c1500 but the church is mentioned in 1316 and 1390. A doorway to a north sacristy remains, and the roof-mark of a porch. A loft stair was made through the east window in the 1720s.

NORTH BERWICK   Lothian   *St Nicholas*   NT 554856   By the harbour

Only the vaulted 16th century south porch now stands complete but there are low walls or footings of the large west tower, the aisled nave and the north transept. The south aisle had an arcade of three bays with square piers but there was just one wide arch into the north aisle, west of which was just a solid wall between it and the nave.

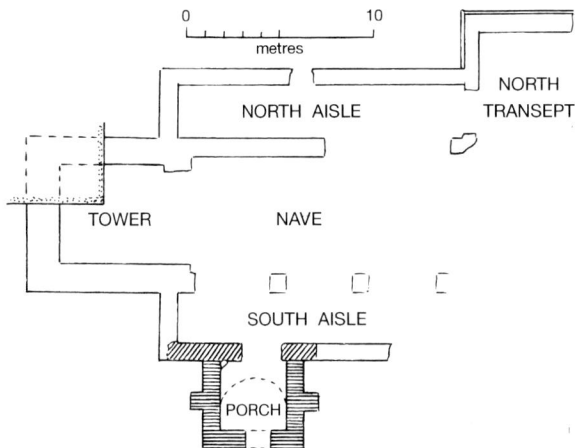

Plan of North Berwick Old Church

ORPHIR   Orkney *St Nicholas*
HY 335043   13km SW Kirkwall

Immediately east of the present church is a tiny vaulted apse with one window and an adjoining fragment of the 7m diameter circular nave of a church thought to have been built by Earl Haakon between a pilgrimage to Jerusalem c1116 and before his death c1122. Six round-naved churches at least partly survive in England but this is the only example known to have existed in any part of Scotland, Wales or Ireland.

PEEBLES   Borders *St Andrew*   NT 245405   At the NW end of the town

After Trinitarian friars took over the original 13th century parish church of St Nicholas of Myra (also known as Crosskirk) in 1474 a new church of St Andrew was built further west. Both churches were burned by the English in 1549. St Andrew's was never repaired and only the west tower (with all its features renewed) and part of the nave north wall now remain. After the friars were dispersed c1561 the nave of the other church (described in Medieval Abbeys and Cathedrals of Scotland) formed the parish church until a new church of St Andrews was built in 1784. See photo on page 75.

PENCAITLAND   Lothian   NT 444690   In village, 11km east of Dalkeith

The NE chapel containing the laird's pew has late 13th century type gabled buttresses but is later medieval. The main body is 16th century work on older foundations. The north transept has initials of Sir John Sinclair on a cartouche over the mid-17th century doorway. The west tower has an octagonal top and is dated 1631 on a lintel.

Orphir: plan
See also page 3

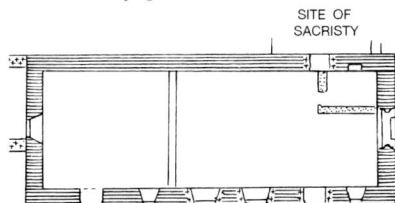

Plan of Newlands Church

Pencaitland Church

PERTH   Perth & Kinross   *St John*   NO 115234   In the centre of the city.

Here in 1286 was buried the heart of Alexander III. In the 1440s Dunfermline Abbey, to whom David I had granted the advowson and tiends of the church c1126, granted funds for the rebuilding of the choir on a much larger scale than previously, resulting in a fully aisled and regularly buttressed structure five bays long. An altar of St John the Evengelist in the north choir aisle was endowed in 1448. The central tower and transepts and an aisled nave also of five bays followed. A view of 1806 shows the upper storey of the north porch as then having a large traceried window, and there were two huge windows in the north aisle east of it. The intention seems to have been for a hall church with aisles as high as the nave, but funds must have proved insufficient and the rest of the north aisle and the south aisle were completed in a more modest fashion as lean-to roofed structures without buttressing or a clerestory. Work on these parts continued until c1500. By that time the church contained as many as thirty altars.

One day after John Knox's sermon in the church against idolatory in May 1559 a mob destroyed many the fittings at St John's before unleashing their fury against the many religious houses in and around the town. The church was subdivided to serve two separate congregations, a 15th century porch (now removed) being transferred here from the Carthusian monastery to enclose a new entrance made in the east wall of the south aisle of the choir. The three west bays of the nave were filled with galleries and then walled off in 1598, and in 1771 the choir was walled off from the crossing create a third separate space for another congregation. The south porch upper room became a session house whilst the north porch upper room was used to imprison prostitutes. The south porch was removed c1800, the north porch upper room was removed c1820, and in 1825 the north transept was shortened to allow road widening.

The interior of the church was finally re-unified in 1923-6 as a war memorial, when new roofs and furnishings were provided, and a new shrine chapel built on the site of a medieval chapel between the north transept and north aisle. Much of the exterior is now 19th and 20th century work, with a new upper stage of the 1920s on the north porch. Some medieval walling remains in the west front and on the north side. The four-light windows of the choir aisles appear to reproduce 15th century originals and one jamb remains of the doorway to a former sacristy on the north side. The arcades contain more 15th century work although some of the octagonal piers have been rebuilt. The SW pier of the central tower contains a spiral staircase.

Interior of St John's Church at Perth

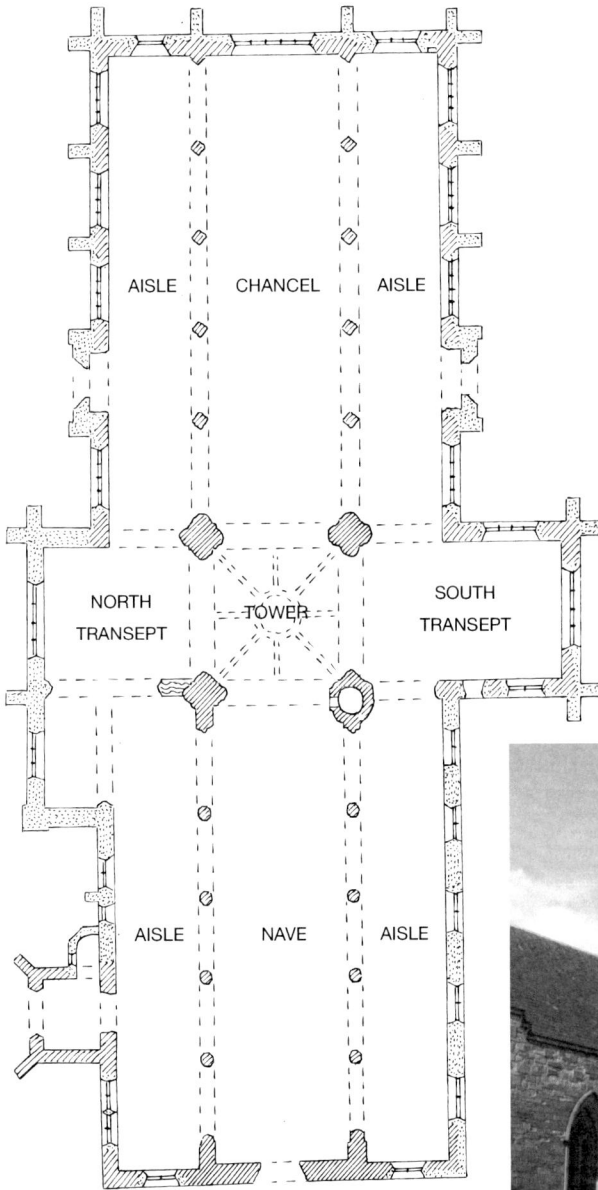

Peebles; Tower of St Andrew's

AISLE CHANCEL AISLE

NORTH TRANSEPT TOWER SOUTH TRANSEPT

AISLE NAVE AISLE

15th Century

Modern

0   metres   10

Plan of St John's Church, Perth

St John's Church, Perth

PETERHEAD   Grampian   *St Peter*   NK 131462   SW corner of the town centre

Of a 12th century church there survive a plain round chancel arch and the side walls with one south window of a chancel which was narrower than the nave and inclined to the south. The east wall does not survive. Only the ends remain of the nave, with a small pyramidal roofed tower at the west end. Most of these parts appear to be 17th century work, a bell in the tower being dated 1647.

PRESTON   Borders   NT 787571   3km north of Duns

The 13th century chancel has twin east lancets and a later window and a piscina on the south. The nave has been converted into burial enclosures, most of the side walls having gone and the doorway is 17th century. The medieval west window is blocked.

PRESTONKIRK   Lothian   *St Baldred*   NT 573779   1km NE of East Linton

At the east end of the plain church of 1770 with windows of the 1890s is the eastern part of the fine 13th century chancel, preserved by the Smeatons as their burial aisle. It has pilaster buttresses and three east lancets of equal height, and another lancet to the south. The high plinth may be a later addition. See plan on page 115.

RATHO   Lothian   *St Mary*   NT 135706   8km SSE of South Queensferry

The nave and chancel both have 12th century cubical masonry and the nave has part of a blocked south doorway with scallop capitals and a hoodmould with sawtooth decoration. The west wall with a blocked lancet and three buttresses appears to be 13th century. The central buttress carries a belfry. The 15th century east window has no tracery but the spandrels between the heads of the lights are pierced. On the north side are two 17th century burial aisles, the eastern one being dated 1683 and opening to the church in a wide segmental arch. The wide south aisle and gallery are of 1830. An 18th century gallery was removed in 1932. The 13th century tomb slab with a cross and sword may commemorate one of the Knights Hospitallers who then held Ratho.

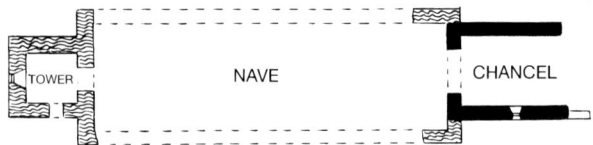

Plan of Peterhead Old Church

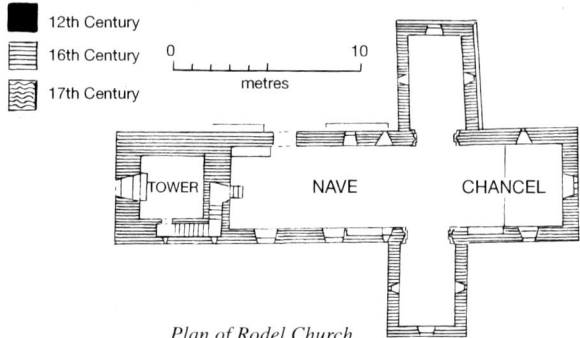

12th Century

16th Century

17th Century

0   10

metres

Ratho Church

Plan of Rodel Church

Rodel: sheila-na-gig

Restalrig Church

The chancel at Prestonkirk

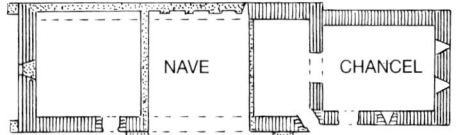
Plan of Preston Church

RESTALRIG   Lothian   NT 283745   2.5km ENE of Edinburgh

The 15th century main body has windows with restored. flowing tracery. The west wall was rebuilt in 1836 and the west porch and the vestry replacing a medieval sacristy are of 1884. By the SW corner is the lower stage of a two storey hexagonal chapel built by James III. It was under construction from c1475 until 1487, when a college was founded here. The lower chapel was dedicated to St Triduana and has a central pier supporting a vault with foliage and shields on the bosses. In 1962 evidence in the form of pier bases was found of an intended aisled choir never actually built.

RODEL   Western Isles   *St Clement*   NG 0478334   At the south corner of Harris

Although modest in scale, this is the grandest church in the Western Isles, and the only one with either a west tower or transepts, those here being set not quite opposite each other. The chancel was probably completed by 1528 when the splendid tomb of Alasdair MacLeod of Dunvegan was set up within it. The tomb has a round-arched recess within a gablet with the Holy Trinity on the keystone. The voussoirs have pairs of Apostles alternating with angels. The effigy has its feet resting on what looks like a crocodile and there are many other carved panels. The effigy of William MacLeod, d1552, lies west of the south transept arch. A more crudely carved effigy in the nave NW corner may be of John MacLeod of Minginish, d1557. The five stage tower is set on higher ground than the nave and has a rope-moulded stringcourse between the third and fourth stages which rises in the middle of each face to frame a carved panel, the motifs being a bishop on the west, a bull on the north, two fishermen in a boat on the east, and a sheela-na-gig on the south. There are trefoil-headed slit windows, the upper ones with hoodmoulds. The crenellated parapet is of the 1780s when the church was restored after being ruinous since the 1580s. New nave windows were then provided. Harling over the walls was removed in 1913. See photo on page 9.

ROSSLYN Lothian *St Matthew* NT 275631 11km south of Edinburgh

William Sinclair, 3rd Earl of Orkney began work on this chapel in the 1440s and es-tablished a college here in 1450. Intended to be about 55m long, the building was ambitiously planned with a fully aisled east end like that of nearby Newbattle Abbey. However the scale of each part was not large and the profuse decorative carving which covers all the parts is more in the nature of encrustation on, rather than an elaboration of, the structural parts. Only the choir 21m long by 10.7m wide and the windowless east walls of the transepts were ever completed. In place of the intended crossing is a tall vestry and organ chamber of 1880. A large medieval sacristy with the Sinclair engrailed cross on its vault lies at a lower level further east. The sixth bay of the choir is an ambulatory off which open a row of four rib-vaulted chapels forming a longer sev-enth bay. The vaults here have saggy-looking pendant bosses. The piers between the ambulatory and the chapels are particularly elaborate, the northern one having eight shafts alternately keeled and covered in leaves, the southern one (the Prentice Pier) having a reeded core and four bands of foliage that twist though 180 degrees.

The main arcade piers are of a complex section and have richly carved capitals above which are a cornice and a clerestory of single-light windows with some size with fleurons on the jambs. There are image niches internally between these windows. The main body has a pointed tunnel-vault and the aisles are covered by a series of pointed tunnel-vaults set crosswise on lintels hidden behind rich encrustations. Upon these vaults again appears the Sinclair engrailed cross. Flying buttresses help to carry the thrust of the main vault onto the aisle buttresses, between which are windows of two lights, although there are doorways under shallow segmental-headed porches in the third bay and the first bay is left blank. The south doorway has three orders of shafts and an ogival hoodmould. The window mullions are twin shafts and there is surface or-namentation of foliage and dogtooth even on the tracery, which is mostly of the flowing type, but with a saltire cross in some windows. There are stone benches between the eastern buttresses, where the pinnacles on top of the buttresses are circular.

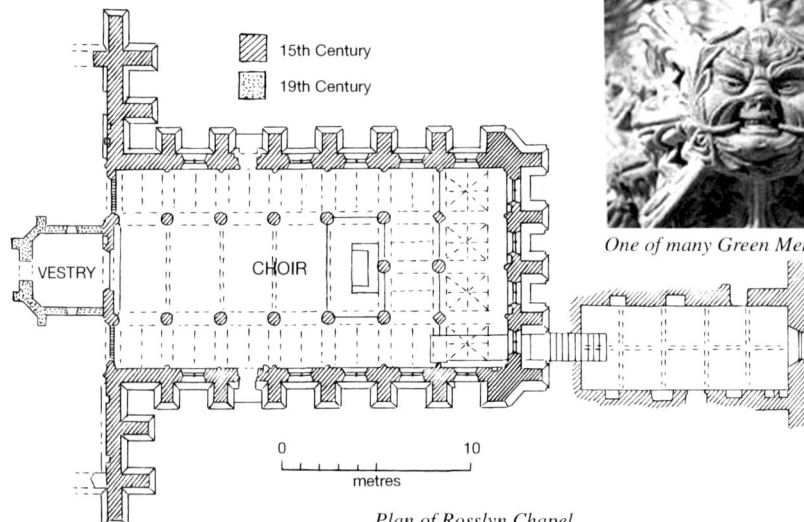

One of many Green Men at Rosslyn

15th Century

19th Century

VESTRY

CHOIR

0   10

metres

Plan of Rosslyn Chapel

Interior of Rosslyn Chapel

Monuments in the chapel include a mid 15th century incised slab of a knight apparently unconnected with the Sinclairs, a tomb of George Sinclair, Earl of Caithness, d1582, and a 13th century coffin lid later inscribed with the name William de Sinclair.

Rothesay, tomb on the south side

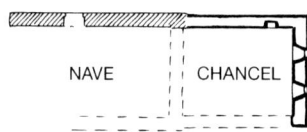

■	12th Century
☐	c1200
▨	15th Century
▤	16th Century

NAVE | CHANCEL

Plan of Rosyth Church

CHANCEL

Rothesay: plan

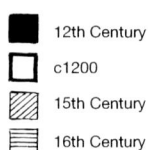

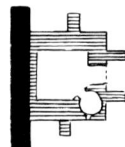

Rutherglen: plan

ROTHESAY   Bute   *St Brioc & St Mary*   NS 086637   0.5km south of town centre

To the SE of the High Kirk of 1796 lies the empty but still roofed 16th century chancel of the medieval church. The north wall has two modest windows and the doorway and the south wall has two small windows and a piscina, whilst the three light east window once had intersecting tracery. An military effigy of one of the Stewarts of Bute lies under an ogival arch on the south side and effigies of a woman and child lie under a canopied round-arched recess opposite on the north side (see photo on page 16).

ROSYTH   Fife   *St John*   NT 085828   2km west of Inverkeithing

Of the ashlar-faced chancel of c1200 there remain the bulging north wall and the east end with two small lancets. Only part of the rubble-built later medieval north wall with a doorway now survives of the nave.

RUTHERGLEN   Lanarkshire   *St Mary*   NS 581628   2.5km SW of Glasgow centre

All that remains of the 13m long chancel demolished in 1793 is the windowless east wall. On the east side of this wall is late medieval tower with buttresses well set-back from the corners, a doorway facing east, and a broach-spire. A church of 1900 lies on the site of the aisled 12th century nave of five bays which was 18.5m long by 14m wide internally. The arcade piers were circular except for the middle pair which were octagonal. Here in 1297 William Wallace concluded a peace treaty with the English forces.

ST ANDREWS Fife *Holy Trinity* NO 509166

Situated on the north side of South Street, this was the parish church of the burgh, begun in 1411. It was heavily restored in 1798-1800 and mostly rebuilt in 1907-9. The western two bays of the arcades are original, and alternate piers further east, and also the tower forming the west bay of the north aisle. It has a recessed spire. There are two bay arcades between the lean-to aisles and the transepts and porch on the south side replacing an original one. There is a fine monument of 1679 to Archbishop Sharp.

In North Street lies a chapel of 1450-60 forming part of Bishop Kennedy's college of St Salvator. It contained his effigy (now lost) and became a commissary court in 1563 and then in 1761 was restored to serve as the parish church of St Leonards. In 1904 it became the University chapel. The chapel has seven bays divided by stepped buttresses towards the street and an east apse. The window tracery is of the 1860s. The fine sacrament house is adorned with a crocket-finialled ogival hoodmould and flying angels holding a pyx. There is an incised slab of a priest.

Holy Trinity Church, St Andrews

ST ANDREWS Fife *St Leonard* NO 511165 SE of city centre

By the early 15th century what was originally the chapel of a pilgrims' hostel had become a parish church. Much of it dates from that period, reusing older stones, but the east two bays were added after an Augustinian college was founded here. In 1761 both the parishioners and students transferred to St Salvator's and St Leonard's was unroofed and its early 16th century west tower demolished, whilst the west bay was removed in the 1830s to improve access to the college buildings then used as houses. The college itself has been a girls' school since 1883.

St Leonard's Church, St Andrews

Tower at Rutherglen

Last remains of St Mary's Church at St Andrews

ST ANDREWS Fife *St Mary* NO 516167 East of both the city and cathedral

Only footings remain of a cruciform church demolished in 1559 and said to have been founded by Constantine II in the late 9th century. The original monastery of the Culdees lay here and my have survived until the church became collegiate and a royal chapel in the 13th century, when transepts and a three bay long new choir were added to a clay-bonded nave perhaps as early as the 10th or 11th century.

ST ANDREWS Fife *St Regulus* NO 515166 East of city, in cathedral precincts

This 11th century church originally had just a two bay long chancel housing the shrine of St Andrew and a slender 33m high west tower acting as a landmark for pilgrims. In the short belfry stage at the top are two-light windows with the central shafts near the outer wall-face. A plain arch of two orders (the inner may be later) leads into the chancel, which has two round-arched windows on each side. Little now remains of the nave west of the tower and a new sanctuary added east of the chancel in the early 12th century. The original chancel appears then to have been heightened. In this form the church served as a cathedral and priory church until the eastern part of the present cathedral begun in 1162 just to the NW was ready to hold services, perhaps in the 1190s. The arch to the new sanctuary has nook-shafts on either side. The arch from the tower to the new nave has the unusual arrangement of two orders side-by-side.

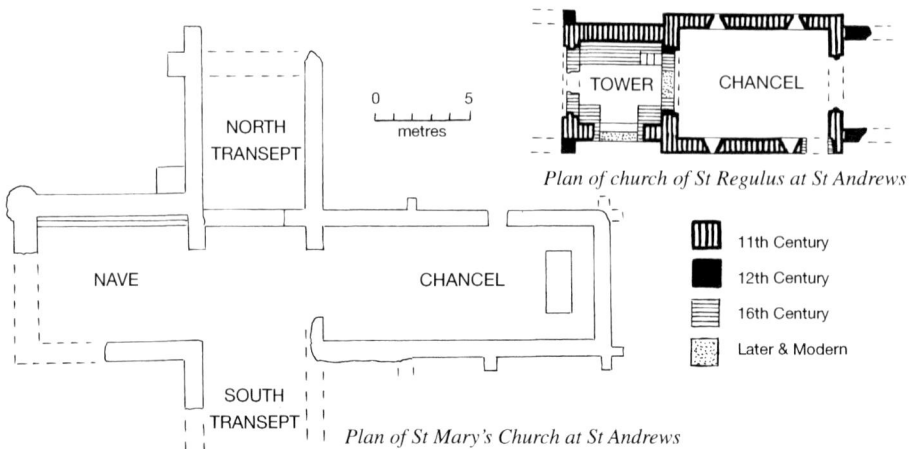

Plan of church of St Regulus at St Andrews

11th Century	
12th Century	
16th Century	
Later & Modern	

Plan of St Mary's Church at St Andrews

St Monans Church

Interior of St Monans Church

ST MONANS   Fife   NO 523014   Just west of the village

This cliff-top church was built at the expense of David II in 1362-70. The rib-vault with heraldic bosses over the choir, and perhaps also the choir windows with rectilinear and curvilinear tracery, date from after James III gave the church to the Dominicans in 1471. The south windows have four lights, the northern ones three and there are two east windows each of two lights. There are three sedilia with ogival arches and a matching piscina and aumbry. In 1647 the choir was closed off from the transepts and fitted out as a parish church. The transepts were only restored from ruin and taken back as part of the church in 1826-8. They were then vaulted but now have wooden ceilings of 1955. The wall closing off the central tower from the intended but soon abandoned nave is partly filled with a circular staircase turret. The short spire is recessed behind a corbelled parapet which was rebuilt in 1899.

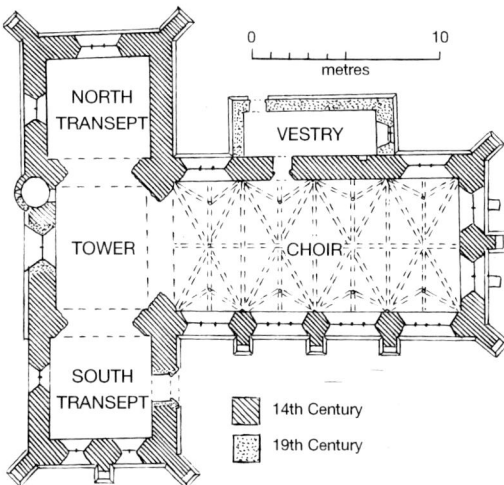

Plan of St Monans Church

St Monans Church

St Vigeans Church

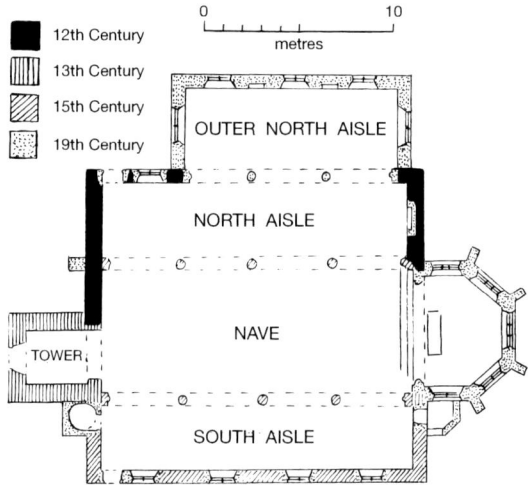

0   10   metres

- ■ 12th Century
- ▥ 13th Century
- ▨ 15th Century
- ▦ 19th Century

OUTER NORTH AISLE

NORTH AISLE

NAVE

TOWER

SOUTH AISLE

Plan of Vigeans Church

ST VIGEANS   Angus   *St Vigeans*   NO 638429   2km north of Arbroath

Parts of the end walls remain of the simple rectangular 12th century church. There was a consecration in 1242 after the addition of a south aisle with a tower projecting west of it. The arcade between the nave and aisle was later moved northwards and they exchanged roles. This may have coincided with the addition of a fresh south aisle with a four bay arcade prior to another consecration in 1485. The polygonal eastern apse, the outer north aisle and the existing windows are all of the time of the restoration of 1872. Inside is a monument to Sir Peter Young, tutor in the 1580s to the young James VI.

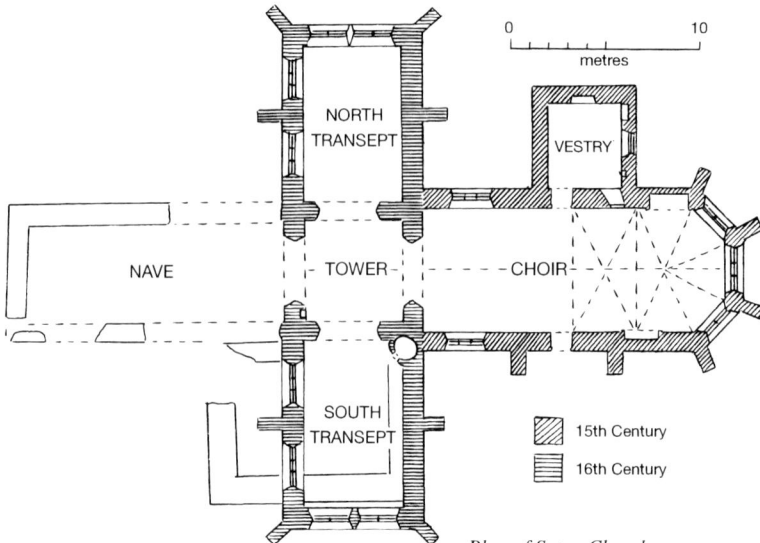

0   10   metres

NORTH TRANSEPT

VESTRY

NAVE

TOWER

CHOIR

SOUTH TRANSEPT

- ▨ 15th Century
- ▤ 16th Century

Plan of Seton Church

Apse interior at Seton Church

Seton Church from the west

SANQUHAR   Dumfries   *St Bride*   NS 779103   At the NW end of the village

In a recess in the church of 1822-4 standing on the site of the nave is an effigy of a priest of c1500. The small figure of a bishop in the porch is still earlier and was found at Dunscore in 1923. The outline of the heavily buttressed chancel was revealed in 1895 and marked out on the ground to the east. It once contained tombs of the Crichtons.

SETON   Lothian   *St Mary & Holy Cross*   NT 418751   3km NE of Tranent

The foundations of the west end of a nave demolished in the 1580s (when the parish was joined to that of Tranent) are all that now remains of a church mentioned here in the 13th century. A large and massively walled south chapel was begun in the 1430s by Catherine Sinclair, wife of the first Lord Seton. In the 1470s the 3rd Lord Seton built a new choir of three bays plus an east apse and a north sacristy. A college was founded by the 4th Lord Seton in 1492 and work continued on the choir vault until c1506. The widow of the 5th Lord Seton (killed at Flodden in 1513) had the south chapel removed in the 1540s to make way for the addition of transepts and a central tower with a spire that was eventually left incomplete.

   The transepts have windows facing west and in the end gables but not facing east. The end windows are of four lights divided into two by an extra large central mullion with Y-tracery. The transepts and the western half of the choir have pointed tunnel vaults whilst the tower and the east part of the choir have ribbed vaults. Slab roofs still remain over the vaults of the transepts and sacristy. The choir has a priests' doorway in the middle bay on the south side and just a single sedile. There are piscinae in the choir and south transept. In the choir are fine effigies of a late 15th century knight and lady, and a fine monument of James, Earl of Perth, d1611 lies in the south transept. There is also a damaged octagonal font bowl with shields on each face.

SKIPNESS Argyll *St Brendan* NR 673077 On Kintyre, 12km SSE of Tarbert

Near the shore SE of Skipness Castle is Kilbrannan Chapel, also late 13th century or early 14th century. Six original worn sandstone lancets remain, plus a two-light east window with Y-tracery, and three doorways, two of them facing south. Three 14th to 16th century tapered memorial slabs with various motifs remain in around the ruin.

SMAILHOLM Borders NS 648364 10km ENE of Melrose

The chancel has two blocked 12th century windows facing east and another on the north side. The nave also has 12th century walling but the south doorway, the birdcage bellcote and NW porch (for the gallery doorway) are of 1632. The apsidal transept added in 1820 was only opened to the church in the restoration of 1895. A carved fragment with bands of dogtooth and interlace is 13th century.

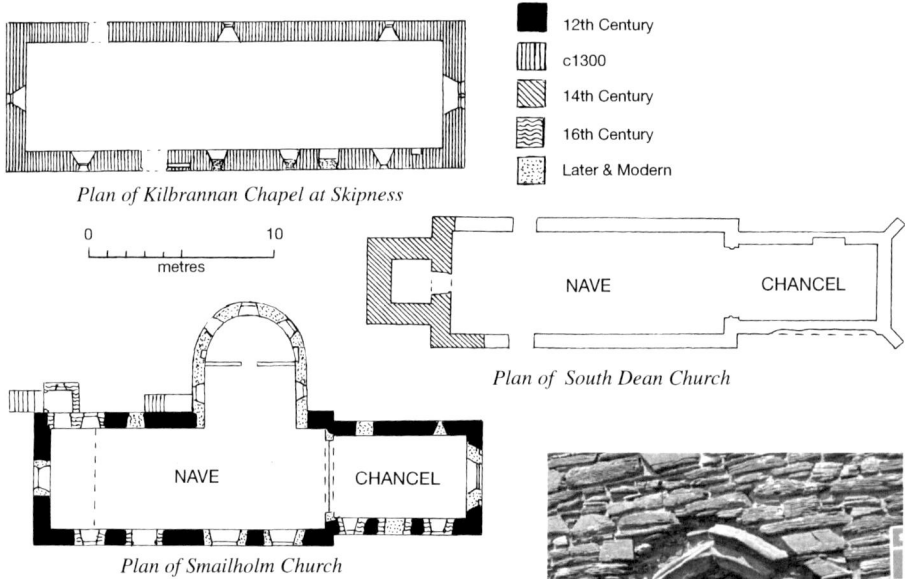

12th Century
c1300
14th Century
16th Century
Later & Modern

Plan of Kilbrannan Chapel at Skipness

0   10
metres

NAVE   CHANCEL

Plan of South Dean Church

NAVE   CHANCEL

Plan of Smailholm Church

Smailholm Church

Kilbrannan Chapel at Skipness

Window from South Leith now in Argyll

South Dean Church

SOUTH DEAN   Borders   NT 631091   12km SSW of Jedburgh

Excavations in 1910 revealed the vaulted basement of a 14th century west tower and footings of a contemporary nave with a narrower and later chancel with diagonal buttresses. A new church was built at Chetwind after the roof here collapsed in 1688.

SOUTH LEITH   Lothian   *St Mary*   NT 270761   2.5km NNE of Edinburgh

Despite having a fully aisled nave, transepts and a chancel, this building of the 1480s ranked only as a chapel until 1609, although it functioned as a parish church after the 1560 bombardment of the town, in which the eastern parts were destroyed. A seven-light window with intersecting tracery was then inserted into the western arch of the crossing. A tower built over the west gable in 1615 was rebuilt in 1674 and demolished as unsafe in 1836. Except for the lower outer walls and arcades most of what now stands dates from a rebuilding of the 1840s which removed two of the galleries. The end galleries still remain. In the NW vestibule are two stone panels. One is dated 1560 with arms of Mary of Guise (from her house in Water Lane). The other is dated 1565 with Queen Mary's arms and was originally part of the town tolbooth. From this church came the six-light window with flowing tracery now at St Conan's, Loch Awe, Argyll.

Old print of South Leith Church before the 1840s

North side of Holy Rude Church, Stirling

STIRLING   Stirlingshire   *Holy Rude*   NS 793936   To NW of town, towards castle

The original 12th century church was repaired in 1414 following fire damage. After probably being damaged again in 1455 during James II's contest with the Douglases the king provided funds for constructing the present five bay aisled nave and the lower stage of the rectangular west tower. The easternmost arcade piers are lozenge-shaped but the other piers and the responds are circular. The capitals have moulded rings, some adorned with foliage. The clerestory only has windows on the south side. The arms of Adam Cosour and Katherine Fotheringham on the western bay of the south aisle octopartite vault suggest that that part was completed in the 1470s. In the 1480s Cosour was one of several wealthy burgesses that began to erect chantry chapels outside of the aisles. St Andrew's Chapel by the north transept remains complete and now contains the oldest memorials (of the 1580s and 90s), plus a font made from a stone carved with tracery patterns from Cambuskenneth Abbey. Only a blocked arch marks where Bowye's Chapel on the south side once stood, and there are footings and another blocked arch of the former St Mary's Chapel at the NW corner.

In 1507 work was begun on the choir after the burgesses made an agreement with Dunfermline Abbey, but it dragged on until the 1540s, by which time the church had been made collegiate. The choir has three bays flanked by vaulted aisles with its much greater height allowing tall four-light windows. It ends in a slightly wider polygonal apse of two bays with huge buttresses necessitated by the fall of the ground at this end. The east windows is of six lights with rectilinear tracery but the other apse windows are smaller openings of three lights. There is a tomb recess in the north aisle. Piers were begun but left incomplete for a central tower which was given up and the west tower built up instead with an embattled square top stage flanked by open parapets. A controversy over the appointment of a second minister in 1656 led to the erection of a partition wall for separate congregations. There were restorations in 1803, 1818, 1869 and 1911-14, but not until 1936-40 were the two parts reunited as one church and the intended transepts finally erected. The existing porch on the south side is modern.

15th Century
16th Century
Later & Modern

APSE

CHANCEL

NORTH TRANSEPT

SOUTH TRANSEPT

NAVE

PORCH

TOWER

0   10
metres

Holy Rude Church, Stirling

Holy Rude Church, Stirling

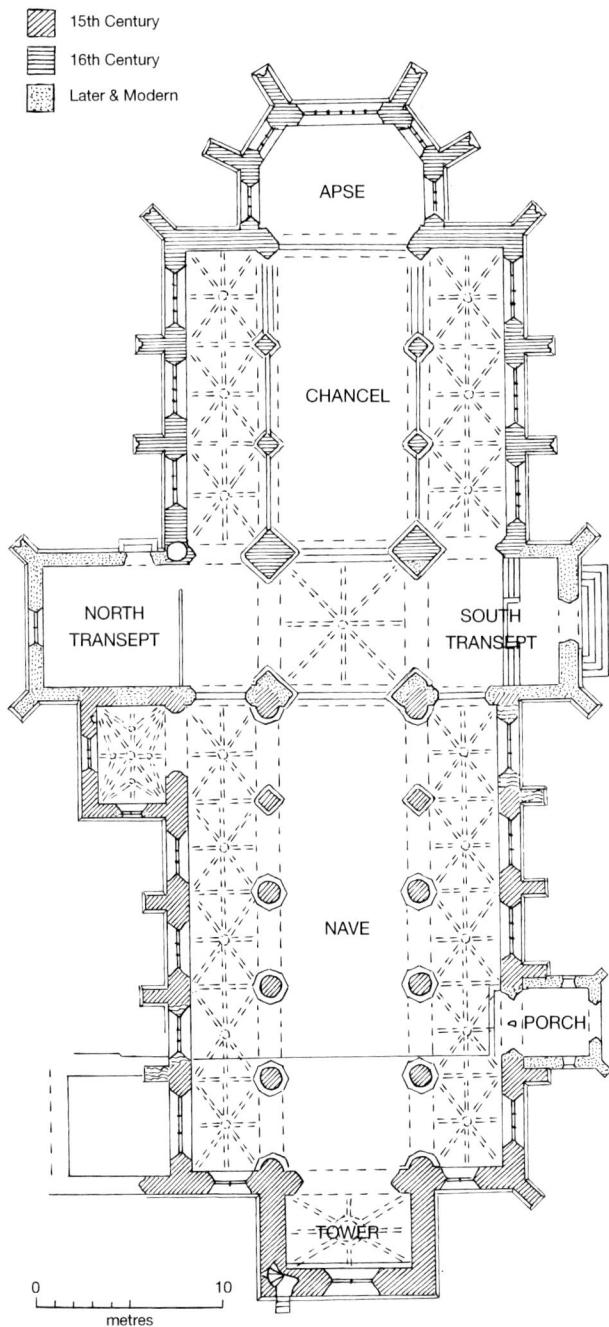

Plan of Holy Rude Church, Stirling

Stobo Church

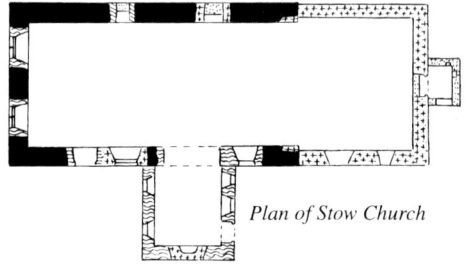

Plan of Stow Church

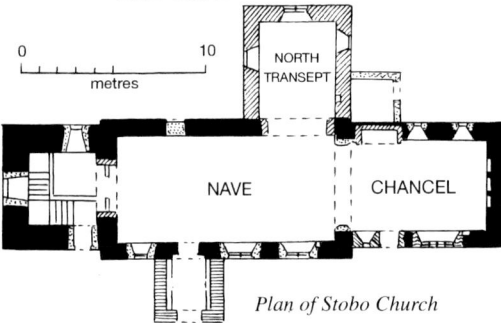

Plan of Stobo Church

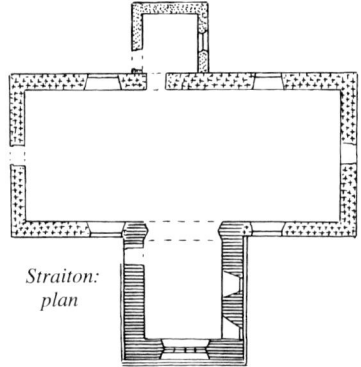

Straiton: plan

STOBO Borders *St Mungo* NT 182376 8km SW of Peebles

Original features of this 12th century church are the tiny east window high up in the chancel and the nave north doorway now converted into a window. Two small north windows in the chancel have been renewed. The massive base of the saddle-back roofed west tower may also be 12th century, but the thinner walling above is 16th century. The chancel SW window is 14th century. The north transept (chapel of St Mary) of the 1460s contains an incised slab of the priest Robert Vesey, d1473. The transept vault is of 1928. It and the chancel were walled off at the Reformation and allowed to decay until the restoration of 1863. The vaulted south porch is 16th century and the four-light south window with intersecting tracery is 17th century.

STOW Borders *St Mary* NT 458444 8km SW of Lauder

The west and north walls are partly 12th century and the blocked round-arched north doorway is older than the date 1714 which appears over it. The chancel was re-roofed in 1541 and rebuilt in a shorter and wider form than before in 1771. The transeptal laird's aisle on the south side is 17th century. The church possessed fragments of an ancient image of the Virgin which attracted pilgrims and lay near a house of the bishops of St Andrews. It was left to decay after a new church was built in the 1870s.

STRAITON Ayrshire *St Cuthbert* NS 380050 9km SE of Maybole

This is the only medieval parish church in the counties of Ayr and Renfrew still in use. The main body was rebuilt in the 18th century and has a north porch of 1901. The ashlar-faced south transept with a four-light window with cusped roundels was built in the 16th century to accommodate a chantry founded in 1350. It was later a laird's loft.

Transeptal chapel at Straiton

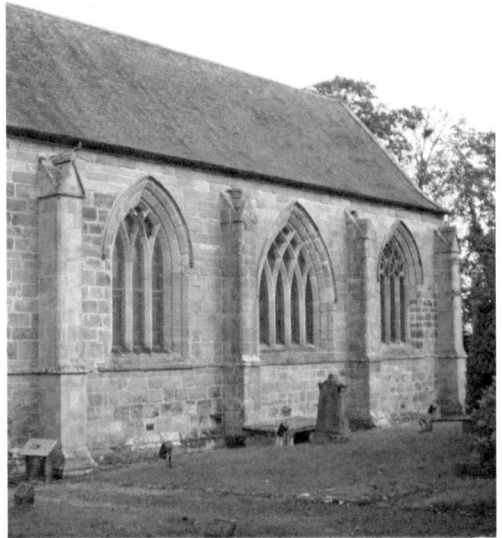

Collegiate church at Tain

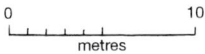

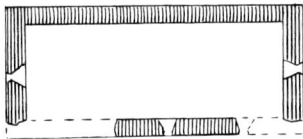

Tain: plan of original parish church

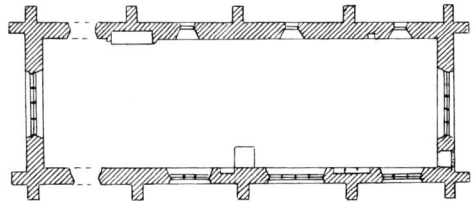

Tain: plan of collegiate church

TAIN   Highland   *St Duthus*   NH 780822   on the north side of the town

The church built to serve the college founded in 1487 by Thomas Hay, Bishop of Ross at the instigation of James III is a wide and still roofed rectangle divided by buttresses into four bays with windows of three and four lights with intersecting tracery on the south side and in the west end. There are opposed doorways in the west bay and east of the northern one is a tomb recess now occupied by pedestal bearing a graveslab depicting a priest. The hoodmould heads of a king and bishop on the south doorway have been renewed. There are sedilia on the south side. A blocked doorway in the SE corner led eastwards to a vestry. The plain octagonal 13th century font came from Suddie on the Black Isle. The much restored pulpit against the south wall was provided in the 1570s when this building took over (until 1815) the function of parish church originally provided by the ruined building with 13th century round-headed west and south facing lancets in the Victorian cemetery 250m to the NE down Chapel road.

Just to the south of the collegiate church is a small ruined chapel with double lancets facing south and a triple lancet facing east. This may be the building burned in 1427 and repaired by 1457 when James II endowed a chaplain to serve it.

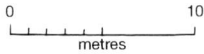

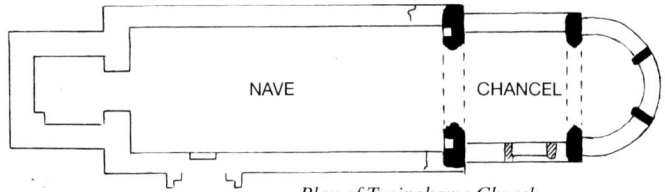

Plan of Tyninghame Church

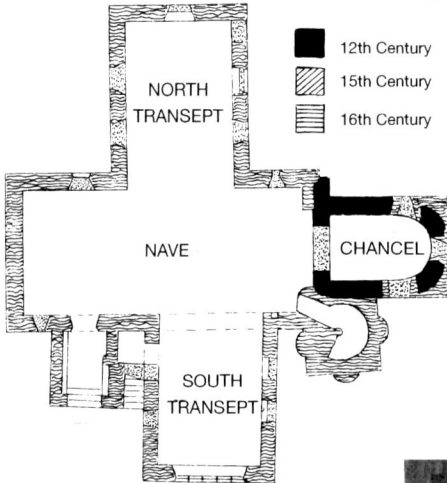

12th Century	17th Century
15th Century	18th Century
16th Century	19th Century

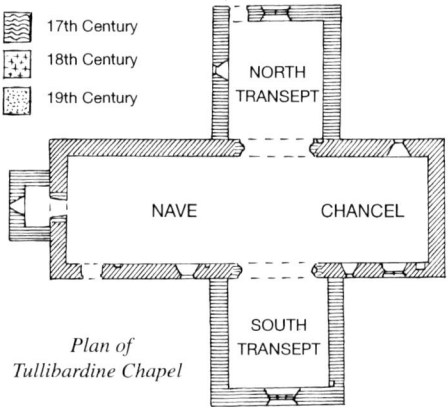

Plan of Tullibardine Chapel

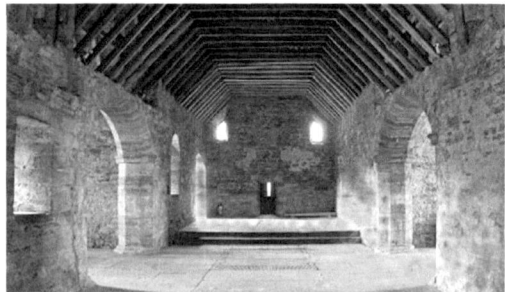

Plan of Thurso Old Church

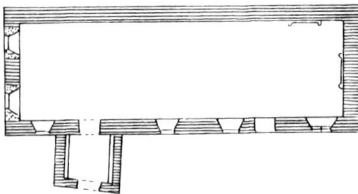

Plan of Tullibody Church

Interior of Tullibardijne Chapel

TEMPLE   Lothian   NS 315588   8km SSW of Dalkeith

The Knights Templar had their main Scottish house here from the mid 12th century un-til their suppression in 1312, but the surviving ruin with intersecting tracery with circles in the windows is thought to date from c1350 or later. There are sedilia on the south side and a tomb recess on the north. The rougher 17th century west end may be built from 12th century materials, possibly from a demolished former west tower.

THURSO   Highland   ND 117683   Near to the bridge in the town centre

The vaulted apsed chancel (now a burial aisle of the Sinclairs of Forss) is 12th century work. The east end is squared off externally. A square tower set diagonally was added against the south side to give access to a session house and court room added over the vault. By then a new nave had been raised on the footings of the medieval one and a south transept added with a porch beside it. The north transept and NE porch were added in 1664. The church has been ruined since a new one was built in 1833.

TULLIBARDINE   Perth & Kinross   NN 900134   4km WNW of Auchterarder

The main body was built to contain a chantry founded in 1446 by Sir David Murray. His arms and those of his wife Margaret Colquhoun appear on a panel which was reset over the north doorway of the northern of two transepts added c1500 by Sir Andrew Murray. Next to the panel is a hood-moulded window of two lights with uncusped loop tracery. More loop tracery appears in the south transept end window of three lights and here there is a corner skewputt with arms of Sir Andrew and his wife Margaret Barclay. Also of c1500 are the tiny west tower and probably the west end of the main body including the finely moulded south doorway. The east end has a restored two-light window facing south and a small east window recessed for shutters set high up. The roofs are mainly original. The chapel later served as a parish church until 1745 and survived in use as the Murray burial place until taken into state care.

TULLIBODY   Stirlingshire   *St Mungo*   NS 860954   3km NW of Alloa

The walls of cubical ashlar are mostly 12th century except for the windowless east wall of rubble which is later. The rectangular windows and the two doorways on the south side appear be of 1539, that date together with a crozier appearing on the eastern doorway lintel. East of it is a two-light window with more elaborate mouldings. The church roof was taken off in 1560 by French soldiers to make a bridge over the River Devon. It was only replaced c1760 to provide the Abercrombies with a mausoleum. The building was restored and again re-roofed in 1833 to serve as a chapel-of-ease to Alloa. The church was again unroofed in 1916 after a new church was built in 1904.

TYNINGHAME   Lothian   *St Baldred*   NT 620798   4km NE of East Linton

In the grounds of the house are foundations of a 12th century church dismantled after the laird cleared the away the village in 1761. It had a west tower, a long nave with a wide and boldly projecting south doorway, a square choir and an apse. The arches to the choir and apse still stand, and also the shafts which carried the apse vault. These parts are richly ornamented with chevrons, billets and lozenges.

Plan of Temple Church

Tullibody Church

Tyninghame Church

Uphall Church

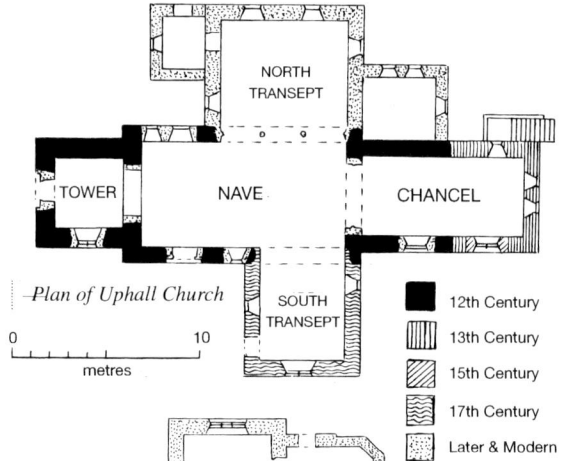

Plan of Uphall Church

0   10

metres

■	12th Century
▥	13th Century
▨	15th Century
≈	17th Century
∴	Later & Modern

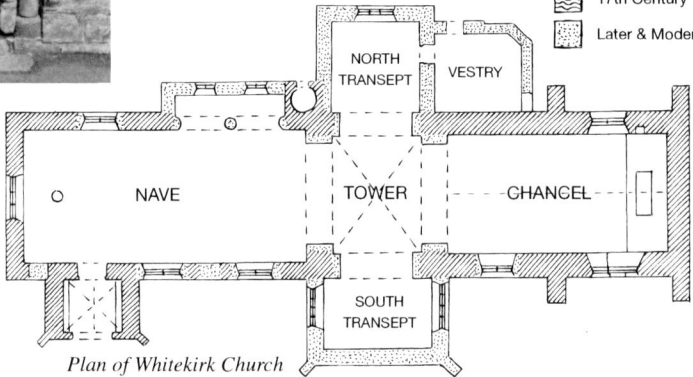

Plan of Whitekirk Church

UPHALL   Lothian   *St Nicholas*   NT 060722   7km SE of Linlithgow

The west tower, nave and chancel all have 12th century masonry and there is a good doorway with old order of shafts. The chancel was lengthened in the 13th century and had one north lancet and two eastern ones of that period, plus a 15th century south window of two lights. The Sharps of Houston added a tunnel-vaulted south transept c1620. Only a staircase remains of the burial vault and loft of the Buchans on the north side of the chancel. The north transept and vestry and the tower top are of 1878. The late medieval octagonal font basin now lies in the Catholic church at Broxburn.

WHITEKIRK   Lothian   *St Mary*   NT 596815   4km north of East Linton

In the 15th century Whitekirk was an important place of pilgrimage because of miracles of healing at a nearby well. Pilgrims's hostels were built in the 1430s by James I and the church was rebuilt to a cruciform plan with a central tower. The two bay chancel with a plain pointed tunnel vault, one original three-light south window and a blank east wall except for a renewed occulus high up is said to be the work of Adam Hepburn of Hailes in the 1430s, but the shield on the east wall is that of Abbot Crawford of Holyrood (1460-83). The north transept was rebuilt at some unknown period and the south transept was rebuilt in 1830 and again along with the crossing arches after the church was gutted by a fire started by suffragettes in 1914. Many fine 17th century furnishing were lost in the fire. The south porch retains original inner and outer arches.

0   10
metres

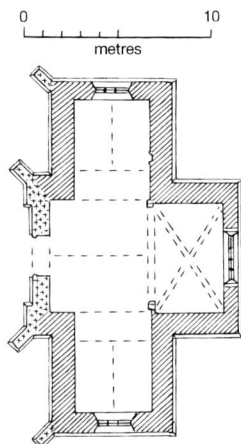

Plan of Yester Church

Whitkirk Church

YESTER   Lothian   *St Cuthbert*   NT 545672   8km SSE of Haddington

Hidden in shrubs near Yester House is a burial chapel formed from the eastern parts of the former church which was consecrated in 1241 by David de Bernham, Bishop of St Andrews, but entirely rebuilt after being made collegiate in the 15th century. It had a short and slightly narrower sanctuary at the east end which was given a new east window in 1633 and later divided off by a thin arch. Low round arches lead into transepts, which have lofty pointed vaults like that of the main body. A new church was built at Gifford in 1710 and in 1753 everything west of the transepts at the old church was removed and a new Gothick style screen wall built by the Adam brothers.

FURTHER READING

Buildings of Scotland series, various authors: Lothian 1978, Edinburgh 1984, Fife 1988, Glasgow 1990, Highlands and Islands 1992, Dumfries & Galloway 1996, Argyll and Bute 2000, Stirling and Central Scotland 2002, Borders 2006, Perth and Kinross 2007.

Royal Commission on Ancient and Historical Monuments of Scotland inventories: Caithness 1911, Sutherland 1911, Wigtown 1912, Kirkcudbright 1914, Berwick 1915, Dumfries 1920, East Lothian 1924, The Outer Isles 1924, Mid & West Lothian 1929, Fife, Kinross & Clackmannan 1933, Orkney and Shetland, 1946, Roxburgh 1956, Selkirk, 1957, Stirling, 1963, Peebles 1967, Argyll 1971-92.

The Ecclesiastical Architecture of Scotland, David McGibbon and Thomas Ross, 3 volumes 1897, facsimile reprint 1985.

The Queen's Scotland, Nigel Tranter, three volumes: The Heartland 1971, The Eastern Counties, 1972, The North East, 1974

Scottish Medieval Churches, Stewart Cruden, 1986

Scottish Medieval Churches, Richard Fawcett, 1985

The Architecture of Scotland, J.G.Dunbar, 1966

Medieval Scotland, Peter Yeoman, 1995

OTHER CHURCHES: ABERDEENSHIRE & MORAY

ABERDOUR NJ 884645 Tomb recess amongst burial enclosures in east end of the 16th century main body. Long laird's aisle on south side is 16th or 17th century.

ABERLOUR NJ 266430 Only the west wall remains of narrow church of St Drostan.

ALFORD NJ 554161 Church of 1804 on site of church of Andrew rebuilt in 1604.

ALVAH NJ 670610 Footings of chapel of St Colm. Panel of 1589 at later church.

ALVES NJ 126639 Cross-shaft at farm on or near site of medieval parish church.

AUCHENBLAE NO 727784 Regular south fenestration suggests a post-Reformation date, but the piscina must be a relic of chapel of St Palladius consecrated 1244.

BANCHORY NO 706959 Church of St Ternan rebuilt 1775. New church nearby 1824.

BANCHORY NO 906025 Church of St Devenick rebuilt 1822. Bell of 1597.

BANFF NJ 688837 Fragment of north wall with tomb recess. Burial aisle of 1580 for monuments to parents of Sir George Ogilvie of Dunlugas on south side.

BELHELVIE NJ 969197 Gable and one other fragment of uncertain date.

BELLIE NJ 354610 Fragment only of St Ninian's Church, with Dunbar monument.

BIRSE NJ 554974 Good 13th century cross-slab in porch of church of 1779.

BOHARM NJ 321465 Only the west wall with a blocked doorway now remains.

BOTRIPHNIE NJ 375441 Part of south wall with blocked arch into later burial aisle.

BOURTIE NJ 804249 Effigies of 14th century knight and wife in porch of church of St Brandon rebuilt in 1806. Part of Pictish symbol-stone built into top of south wall.

BRAEMAR NO 153922 Farquharson mausoleum on site of church of St Andrew.

BROADSEAT NJ 709210 Foundations only of tiny medieval chapel.

CAIRNIE NJ 489447 Pitlurg aisle dated 1597 with effigy by site of St Martin's church.

CLATT NJ 539260 Old font in church of 1799. Descriptions alone exist of the former piscina, sacrament house and a coloured panel depicting the crucifixion.

COULL NJ 511024 Founded by St Nathalan, d678. Rebuilt 1792. Bell of 1642.

CRATHIE NO 265947 16th century ruin near church of 1890 used by royal family. Older church stood by standing stone at Rinabaich at NO 301962.

CRIMOND NJ 053576 Part of south wall survives with two windows and door jamb.

CULSAMOND NJ 650330 Possible fragment of older church by 17th century ruin.

DALLAS NJ 122519 Church of 1793 has old cross. Replaced church of St Michael.

DRUMBLADE NJ 589402 Church of St Hilary replaced by one of 1773 and 1829.

DRUMDELGIE NJ 487410 Foundations and part of west wall of church of St Peter. Also known as the Brunt Kirk, because of an accidental fire in the 16th century.

DRUMOAK NO 815985 St Moluag. SW and west doorways with drawbar-slots may be medieval. Outside staircases and other openings in south wall are 17th century.

Tomb-recess at Aberdour

Plan of Dyce Church

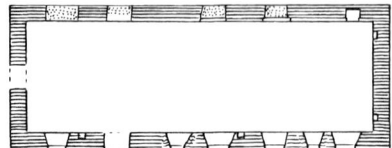

Plan of Deskford Church

DYCE NJ 877155 Church of St Fergus retains original east window, blocked south
doorway and sill of sacrament house. Old font and two Pictish symbol stones.
DYKE NH 991584 East end, now vestry over crypt, may be 15th century. Rest 1781.
ELLON NJ 959304 Church of 1777, replacing one of St Mary which existed by 1150.
FARSKANE NJ 500672 Cullen Bay Hotel stands on or near site of medieval chapel.
FETTERANGUS NJ 981505 Ivy-covered fragment of church on site of stone circle.
FETTERESSO NO 854857 Church of St Caran dedicated 1246 has two late medieval
opposed doorways, a 17th century north transept and a west doorway of the 1720s
FETTERNEAR A chapel here existed by 1109. Ruin of modern building by River Don.
FINTRAY NJ 872156 Sacrament house in NE corner of otherwise much rebuilt ruin
of church of St Meddan, in use until 1703, now Forbes-Semphill burial enclosure.
FORBES NJ 519169 Thick walled ruin with aumbry and possible tomb recess.
FORGLEN NJ 697499 16th century aumbry and a stone recording a rebuilding in
1652 remain in a later burial enclosure.
FORMASTON NJ 541002 Consecration cross at Aboyne Castle came from here.
FORGUE NJ 611447 Church of 1819 on site of that of St Margaret. Silver cup 1567.
FORRES NJ 035589 Church of St Lawrence of 1775, etc, probably on an old site.
FORVIE NK 021265 Chapel of St Ninian has two opposed doorways and an aumbry.
Piscina found in excavations now in National Museum of Antiquities in Edinburgh.
FYVIE NJ 768378 Church of St Peter rebuilt 1818 has a bell of 1609, a panel of 1603
and four good Pictish inscribed stones found locally built into outside of east wall.
GARIOCH NJ 716241 Church of 1813 on site of chapel of St Mary.
GARTLY NJ 299014 Wing dated 1621 with belfry remains in Kirkstyle graveyard.
GARVOCK NO 744705 St James's chapel held by Arbroath abbey replaced in 1778.
GLENBERVIE NO 766807 Featureless east end now forms a Douglas enclosure.
INSCH NJ 631282 West wall of St Drostan's church, with doorway inserted in 1613.
INVERAVON NJ183376 Three Pictish stones in 1806 successor of St Peter's church.
INVERBERVIE NO 830727 West wall still remains, with a later doorway inserted in it.
A birdcage type bellcote has replaced a corbelled bellcote, probably 16th century.
INVERBOYNDIE NJ 666644 16th century west wall and a burial vault on the north.
INVERURIE NJ 782205 Graveyard beside motte and bailey castle once contained a
12th century church. Several good Pictish symbol-stones still remain.
KEIG NJ 620188 17th century, on site of church of St Diaconianus mentioned 1202.
KEITH NJ 428507 Minor fragments of church of St Maolrubha rebuilt in 1569 and
abandoned 1819. Old drawing shows a central tower and three outside staircases.
KEMNAY NJ 733160 Chapel of St Anne replaced in 1632, and again in 19th century.
KENNETHMONT NJ 539295 Lower parts of north & east walls of church of St Rule.
KILDRUMMY NJ 473177 St Bride. North wall with effigies of a 15th century knight
and wife (see page 15). A join suggests the chancel was enlarged about that time.
KINBATTOCK NJ 429120 Assumed site of original Towie parish church of St Bartha.
KINCARDINE NO 671751 A chapel of St Catherine stood near the castle ruins.
KINELLAR NJ 821144 Old font and a bell of 1615 remain at church rebuilt in 1801.
KING EDWARD NJ 709578 Western part now burial enclosures has 16th century
west doorway and possibly older south window. Tomb recess dated 1590 is all that
remains of chancel. East and west walls of 16th century south transept also remain.
KINNEFF NO 856749 Church consecrated in 1242 rebuilt in 1738 except maybe the
west wall. Formerly had eight buttresses and a wooden arcade. Here the Honours
of Scotland lay hidden from 1652 until the restoration of Charles II in 1660.

LEOCHEL CUSHNIE NJ 506108 Featureless remains of former church of St Bride.
LESLIE NJ 596239 Site of old chapel. Font said to be buried under an outbuilding.
LOGIE DURNO NJ 704264 Ivy-covered heaps of rubble mark out extent of church.
LOGIE MAR NJ 436024 Site of church of St Walloch given to St Andrews in 1153.
LUMPHANAN NJ 594049 Church of 1782 and 1851 on site of that of St Finan.
MARNOCH NJ 598501 1792 church close to minor remains of that of St Marnoch.
MARYKIRK NO 686656 Piscina in Strachan burial enclosure dated 1615 over door.
MELDRUM NJ 786312 Minor remains of Belnathie parish church of St Nathalan.
    There was also once a medieval chapel at Chapelhouses to south at NJ 809301.
METHLICK NJ 858373 Ruin of uncertain date on site of old church of St Devenick.
MIDMAR NJ 702059 Remains divided up as burial enclosures. Large east window.
MIGVIE NJ 437069 Good Pictish stone at church of 1777 replacing that of St Finan.
MONYKEBBOCK NJ 876181 Footings of chapel of St Colm in walled circular grave-
    yard. A plaque proclaims it was in use from 1256 until 1609. Other old chapels
    stood on the estates of Parkhill 5km to the SE and Straloch 3km to the NW.
NEWBURGH NK 004256 Udny vault on site of 13th century chapel of Holy Rood.
NEWHILLS NJ 870093 Farm on site of medieval chapel. Ruin of 1663 to the east.
OGSTOUN NJ 194689 Michaelkirk of 1703 lies on site of medieval parish church.
OLD DEER NJ 989477 Eastern part of 12th century nave used as burial enclosure
    has an aumbry containing a stone dated 1603 and a late medieval tomb recess.
RAFFORD NJ 060562 West wall and fragment of south wall beside aisle of 1640.
RATHEN NK 000610 St Ethernan. Long transeptal Fraser burial aisle dated 1646
    adjoins south wall. West wall and doorway of medieval church also still survive.
RATHVEN NJ 444656 Burial vault 1612. Main body mostly rebuilt and much ruined.
RATTRAY NK 085576 13th century chapel of St Mary with damaged triple lancets.
    Also west and south lancets and traces of opposed north and south doorways.
RHYNIE NJ 499265 Tomb recess with coffin beside it. Font at new church in village.
ROTHES NJ 277493 Slight remains of medieval church of St Lawrence.
ROTHIEMAY NJ 547484 Church of 1807 has a font and an arched doorway under an
    angel's head and wings from former medieval chapel of St Drostan by the castle.
RUTHVEN NJ 506468 North and west walls remain, without features except for a
    military effigy of c1400 in a north recess. Bell dated 1643 in west bellcote.
ST COMBS NK 06632 Fragment of St Columba's church abandoned in 1607.
ST CYRUS NO 747649 Burial vault with 17th century doorway may represent chancel

Rattray Chapel

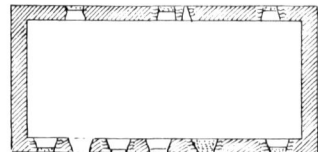

Plan of St Fitticks Church

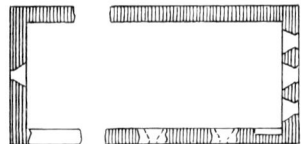

Plan of Rattray Chapel

ST FERGUS NK 116508 Two walls (one with aumbry) of chancel. Abandoned 1616.
ST FITTACKS NJ 963049 Rere-arches of north and south doorways look medieval,
    but the regularly planned windows must now all be 17th century or later.
SEGGAT NJ 728428 Fragment of medieval chapel near holy well of St Mary.
SKENE NJ Church of 1801 on site of St Bride's, once held by a St Andrews college.
SLAINS NK 030326 St Fidamnan's Chapel. Opposed doorways and big east window
    There was probably also a medieval church at Kirkton of Slains (NK 041290).
STRICHEN NJ 947547 Vault and loft of 1620 with adjoining fragments of south wall.
TARLAND NJ 483047 17th century ruin on site of church of St Mathulock or Molluag
TARVES NJ 869312 St Englatius. Forbes aisle of 1589 with tomb. Main body gone.
TULLICH NO 390975 Blocked medieval north doorway. South windows 17th century
TURRIFF NJ 729497 36m long church with west end missing. Features of later date.
See also entries for: Aberdeen, Altyre, Arbuthnott, Birnie, Cowie, Cullen Deskford,
    Fordyce, Gamrie, Kincardine, Kinkell, Mortlach, Peterhead, Ruthven
Also still in use as parish churches: Aberdeen Cathedral & Monymusk Priory Church
Later churches on medieval sites: Glenbuchat NJ 376162, Kintore NJ 793163,
    Logie Buchan NJ 98929), Old Rayne NJ 698302, Ordiquhill NJ 56555,
    Oyne NJ 682257, Peterculter NJ 842003, Premnay NJ 643251
Graveyard marks site of church: Daviot NJ 749283, Dunbennan NJ 504409, Echt
    NJ 739052 Elchies NJ 279442 Essie NJ 466279, Kineddar NJ 223694, Kirkmichael
    NJ 143239, Lhanbryde NJ 269613, Portsoy NJ 594661, Udny NJ 880264
Farm on or near site: Chapelton NJ 584371, Dipple NJ 329570, Essil NJ 340635,
    Nether Towie NJ 447119 St Andrews NJ 248629, Tillygreig NJ 866230
Other sites: Aboyne NJ 541001, Glenmuick NO 365949, Kinnoir NJ 544432

*Note: Most places with little
or no standing medieval walls
are not included on this map,
except those with significant
other features such as effigies.*

Memorial slab at Kinkell

OTHER CHURCHES: ANGUS

ABERLEMNO NO523556 Older work in church of 1722. Rope-moulded font now in manse garden. Very fine Pictish slab in churchyard. Three more lie by the roadside.

AIRLIE NO 313516 Now mostly of 1781 but the east vestibule contains a sandstone medieval aumbry with a depiction of the Five Wounds of Christ.

ALDBAR NO 573583 Burial enclosure on site of church abandoned in 17th century.

BENVIE NO 327315 Part of a gable and a broken font are reported to survive here.

CARMYLIE NO 548426 17th century on foundations of medieval church of St Mary.

DUN NO 664600 Ruin of 1840 on site of chapel. Another stood to east near Kirkhill.

EASSIE NO 353474 Ivyclad ruin of uncertain date. Fine Pictish slab within.

EDZELL NO 582688 Only relic of church of St Laurence is the Lindsay burial aisle with ogee-headed piscina, representing former chancel or built out of its materials.

ETHIE NO 705480 Featureless gable alone remains of clifftop church of St Murdoch.

FERN NO 484616 Tiny church of St Ninian was rebuilt in 1806. Dated bell of 1506.

FORFAR NO 456505 18th century church on site of St James's Chapel of 1241.

GLAMIS NO 386469 Church of St Fergus on 8th century site consecrated in 1242. Cross-slab in church of 1973. North transept 1732. Carnegie vault dated 1636.

INCHBRAYOCK NO 707568 Burial enclosure of the Scotts of Rossie may include material from the church of St Brioc which was ruinous by 1573.

INVERGOWRIE NO 351301 Medieval south doorway and trefoil-headed window. Two fragmentary stones go back to period of St Boniface who landed here c715.

INVERKEILOR NO 664496 Main body appears now to be all of 1830 and 1862.

KETTINS NO 238390 Culdee monastery until given to Coupar Angus Abbey in 1249. Once had chapels of ease at Denhead, Muiryfaulds, Peatie, Pitcur, South Corston. Rebuilt 1768. Pictish slab, old cross, old font, bell dated 1519 from a Dutch abbey.

Plan of Old Pert Church

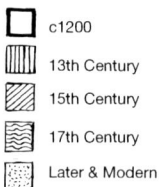

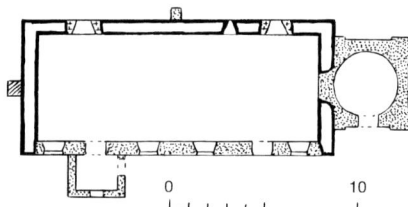

☐	c1200
▥	13th Century
▨	15th Century
▧	17th Century
⬚	Later & Modern

0   10

Plan of Lundie Church

Edzell: burial aisle

Invergowrie Church

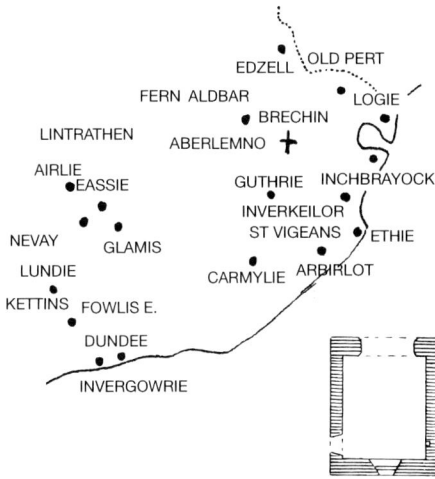

Edzell: plan

Old Pert Church

KINETTLES NO 422467 Church of 1812 replaced a medieval building.

KINNELL NO 609502 Church of 1855 (bell of 1624) on site of St Maelrubha's church.

KIRRIEMUIR NO 386539 Cruciform medieval building replaced by church of 1786.
    Pictish cross-slabs now removed to a shelter in cemetary on hillside to NE.

LIFF NO 333328 Medieval font by church of 1839, third on this site since the 1120s.

LINTRATHEN NO 285546 Pictish stone and old grave-slabs by church of 1802.

LUNAN NO 688516 Possibly old walling in church of 1844. Two old but later panels.
    In 1558 local priest Walter Mill was burned at St Andrews for turning Protestant.

LUNDIE   NO 291366 North wall of small church of St Lawrence has a narrow lancet
    of c1200 and blocked 18th century windows. East apse was removed in 1786.

MENMUIR NO 534643 Church of St Aidan replaced in 1767 and again in 1842.

MONIFIETH NO 495323 St Rule's of 1813 on a site occupied by Culdees to 1242.

MONTROSE NO 714577 Church of 1791 on site of 13th century church of St John.

MURROES NO 461350 North aisle 1642. Medieval main body replaced in 1848.

NEVAY NO 312441 Tiny roll-moulded west window probably 16th century. The
    other openings look later. The date 1597 appears on a slab.

OLD PERT NO 644660 The two east windows, the single west lancet and perhaps
    the doorways are 13th century. The blocked south windows are 17th century.

PANBRIDE NO 571358 17th century vault of earls of Panmure lies at east end.
    Rest of St Bride's church remodelled 1681 and 1775 and rebuilt 1851.

RESCOBIE NO 509520 Rebuilt 1820, but has bell of 1620, on medieval site.

RUTHVEN NO 285489 Painting in church of 1857 shows long low medieval church.

STRATHCATHRO NO 617658 Old stone coffins by church of St Brule rebuilt in 1799.
    Here in 1296 Edward I of England stripped John Balliol of the Scottish kingdom.

TANNADICE NO 475581 Rebuilt 1846 but old font still remains.

See also main gazetter entries: Dundee, Fowlis Easter, Guthrie, Logie and St Vigeans.

Other medieval churches appear to have once stood at: Arbirlot, Barry, Cortachy,
    Dunniechen, Farnell, Finavon, Fintry, Fotheringham, Kingoldrum, Letham, Maryton,
    Monikie, Newtyle, Strathmartine, and Tealing,

OTHER CHURCHES: ARGYLL, BUTE & DUMBARTON

ARDCHATTAN NM 970353 Late medieval church of St Modan on crag NW of priory.
  East window flanked by aumbries. Ragged holes of south window and doorway.
CARA NR 641443 Chapel with a window and two doorways, one with drawbar-slot.
EILEAN MOR NR 666752 c1350 John, Lord of the Isles had a pointed vault set upon
  thickened walling added to the east end of chapel of c1200 with blocked doorway.
  Vault has marks of the wicker mat upon which it was laid. Tomb of priest on south.
FASLANE NS 250898 13th century chapel of St Michael. East wall has two lancets
  with heads cut from single stones. North window and aumbry, plus south doorway.
GARVELLACHS NM 640097 Clay-mortared 11th or 12th century church with west
  doorway and east window at head of gully at Eileach an Naoimh. West of gully is
  a fragment of the nave north wall of a two-celled later medieval church.
GIGHA NR 643481 13th century church of St Catan with three original windows
  set around the east end. Several old grave-slabs, one with an armed figure.
GLENBEG NR 752220 Square-headed west window, two south windows and the
  doorway may be 16th century but walling may be older. Ruinous east end is later.
INNIS SEA-RAMHACH NM 973110 Late medieval ruin in 28m square embanked
  enclosure on islet in Loch Awe. North doorway and traces of three windows.
INNISHAIL NN 098244 Very ruinous church on islet in Loch Awe, abandoned 1736.
  Several graveslabs depicting warriors, plus tomb chest panels and altar frontal.
INVERARY NN 094084 Two medieval bench ends and font bowl in Episcopal church.
  Old grave-slabs at site of medieval church at Kilmaliew graveyard 1.3km to NE.
KILBERRY NR 708641 Fragment of a corner of the church of St Berach burned by
  garrison of Kilberry castle in the 1640s lies west of Campbell mausoleum of 1733.
KILBRIDE NM 857257 Ruin of 1706, altered 1744, on site of medieval church of St
  Bridget demolished in 17th century. Old grave-slabs. Cross dated 1516 230m NNE.
KILCHATTAN NM 744090 Church of St Cathan at Luing remained in use until 1735.
  Doorway and window remain on north side. Hole of former rood-beam on south.
KILCHENZIE NR 673248 St Kenneth's church has 13th century chancel with pointed
  headed east window added to a 12th century nave of the same width with one
  round headed south window and a blocked SW doorway. Several old grave-slabs.
KILCHOUSLAND NR 751220 Cliff-top church of St Constantine abandoned in 1617.
  16th century south doorway and windows. 12th century middle part of north wall.
KILCRENAN NN036229 Church of 1771, altered inside 1904, probably has 13th
  century footings and possibly some walling. Several medieval grave-slabs remain.
KILFINAN NR 934788 Main body rebuilt with a belfry 1759, windows 1881. Lamont
  aisle containing cross-slabs probably a 1633 rebuilding of medieval north transept.
KILKIVAN NR 651201 13th century church of St Kevin. North doorway. Two blocked
  windows in rebuilt south wall. Thin later wall and grave-slab collection at east end.
KILLUNDINE NM 579498 Footings only of a small chapel.
KILMARTIN NM 834989 Rebuilt 1601 and replaced 1834-5. Mausoleum perhaps of
  16th century origin contains over eighty medieval cross fragments and grave-slabs.
KILMICHAEL GLASSARY NR 859936 Many old grave-slabs around 19th cent church
KILMORE NM 887249 St Bean's church partly dismantled in 1876 has round-arched
  tomb recess. Blocked 17th century north windows and west doorway. Porch 1838.
KILMORICH NN189129 Old grave-slab beside site of church of St Muireadhach.
KILNEVAIR NM889036 St Columba. 13th century east end has a piscina and window
  jamb. West end later medieval. Old font, three grave-slabs and tomb-chest panels.
LACHLAN NS 010951 15th century east wall forms west end of MacLachlan burial
  aisle of the 1590s in which are medieval grave-slabs. There is also a` cross-shaft.

LISMORE
ARDCHATTAN
DUNSTAFFNAGE
KILBRIDE
TAYNUILT
KILCRENAN
KILMORE
INNISHAIL
KILCHOUSLAND
INNIS SEARAMHACH
KILMORICH
KILCHATTAN
GARVELLACHS
INVERARY
ST CATHERINE'S
CRAIGNISH
KILNEVAIR
LOCHGOILHEAD
ST BRIDE'S
LACHLAN
FASLANE
KILMICHAEL
LOCH
RIDDON
KILMUN
KEILLS
ST COLUMBA
CARDROSS
DUMBARTON
KILMORY
KILFINAN
EILEAN MOR
OLD KILPATRICK
ROTHESAY
KILBERRY
GIGHA
SKIPNESS
ST BLANE'S
KILLEAN
CARA
KILCHENZIE
LAMLASH
GLENBEG
KILKIVAN
KEIL
SANDA

ten miles

Plan of Faslane Chapel

Plan of Kilmacnaughton Church

Plan of Kilmory Church

East windows at Faslane

LAMLASH NS 033323 Only ancient church on Aran. 14th century north wall with one window and blind east wall. South wall rebuilt in the 17th century.

LOCHGOILHEAD NN 198014 Medieval main body with tomb recess on north. Aisle and doorways are 18th century, windows and session house on south are later. Monument to Sir James Campbell, d1592, Comptroller of Royal Household 1584-5.

LOCH RIDDON NS 021765 Low featureless walls of a small chapel of uncertain date.

OLD KILPATRICK NS 464731 Low relief military effigy by doorway of church of 1812.

ST BRIDE'S NR 851966 13th century chapel with SW doorway and two east lancets.

ST CATHERINE'S NN121073 Foundations excavated 1902 of chapel founded c1460.

ST COLUMBA NR 751767 Fragment of 13th century chapel near to two caves.

ST FILLANS NS 384689 Dated 1635 over doorway but probably older masonry.

SANDA NR 727045 St Ninian's Chapel has a lintelled doorway and one window.

TAYNUILT NN005309 Late medieval. Tomb recess between windows on south side.

Dunoon, Kilmelford, Kilninver, Rosneath and Rossdhu also had medieval churches. See main gazetteer entries for: Bute, Cardross, Dumbarton, Dunstaffnage, Keil, Keills, Killean, Kilmory, Kilmun, Rothesay, and Skipness

OTHER CHURCHES: AYRSHIRE AND THE CLYDE VALLEY

ALLOWAY NS 330180 Twin lancet window and north doorway may be 16th century. Other features of 1653. On Robert Burns trail, being the burial place of his father.

ARDROSSAN NS 233423 Foundations probably of c1270-1300 east of castle ruin.

CARSTAIRS NS 939462 T-shaped 15th century stone with Crucifixion scene, and a second old stone lie in vestibule of church of 1794 altered in 19th centrury.

COULTER NS 028343 Restored late medieval burial aisle added to church founded in 1170, but now replaced by new church of 1810.

COYLTON NS 422194 Later belfry on west gable of c1200. 15th century tomb recess on north side near east end and chamfered arch of former transept on south side.

CUMBERNAULD NS 758748 Church of St Ninian of 1659 on or near medieval site.

DUNDUFF NS 263159 Featureless lower walls of plain rectangle of uncertain date.

EAST KILBRIDE NS 636545 Fragments of medieval church of St Bride may remain in present building dated 1774 over tower doorway. Tower crown is later.

FULLERTON NS 345295 Chapel with small east and south windows and a round-arched south doorway probably of the 16th century.

GLASGOW NS 595649 The Tron Steeple of 1637 is a relic of the collegiate church of St Mary and St Anne built in 1480s, rebuilt 1592, and burnt down by the local Hellfire Club in 1793. The arches under the tower date only from 1855.

GLASSFORD NT 732470 Just west wall and a fragment of north wall now remain.

GOVAN NS 552658 Good collection of Early Christian tomb-stones, crosses and a fine 10th or 11th century sarcophagus on the site of a church of St Constantine.

HOUSTON NS 410670 Monument of Sir Patrick Houston, d1456, and wife Agnes.

KILMACOLM NS 359700 East end of 13th century chancel with triple east lancets now forms a SE vestry of later church. See page 7.

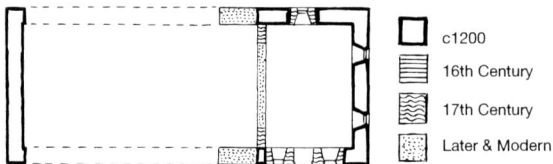

Plan of Loudon Church

- ☐ c1200
- ☰ 16th Century
- ▨ 17th Century
- ▨ Later & Modern

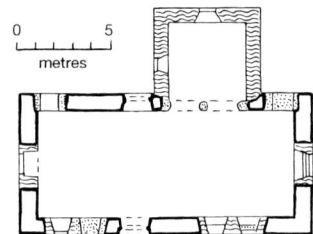

0   5
metres

Plan of Monkton Church

Alloway Old Church

Loudon Church

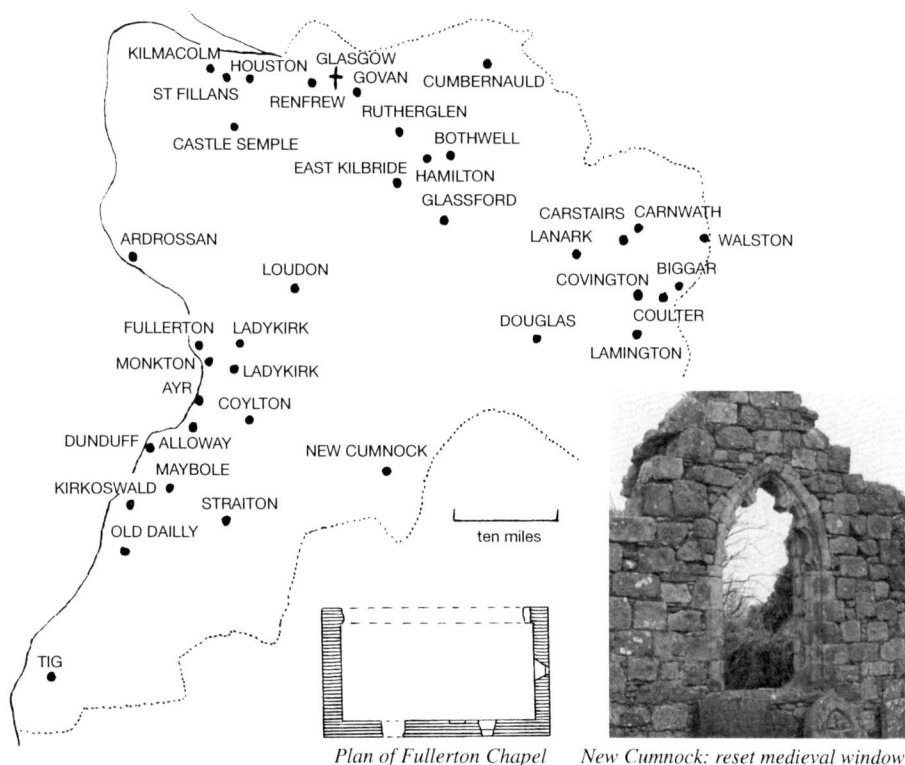

Plan of Fullerton Chapel   *New Cumnock: reset medieval window*

KIRKOSWALD NS 240076 Possible medieval masonry in St Oswald's church, but present features 17th century and of c1800. Church lies on the Robert Burns Trail.

LADYKIRK NS 406299 16th century church of St Mary on hill near Tarbolton has remains of north and south doorways and small east and south windows.

LOUDON NS 493373 West wall plus the eastern third (now a burial vault) of church of c1200 with two small and widely spaced east lancets.

MONKTON NS 357277 Much altered chapel of St Cuthbert remained in use to c1800. Two original opposed round arched and moulded doorways of c1200.

NEW CUMNOCK NS 617137 Remains of good three-light window of c1500 reset in new T-plan church of 1657.

OLD DAILLY NX 226994 26m long church of St Michael perhaps 14th century but much altered. Blocked doorway and south windows late 16th or 17th century.

RENFREW NS 508678 Late medieval tomb of Sir John Ross lies in rebuilt church.

TIG NS 116838 Foundations only of nave and chancel later extended westwards.

WALSTON NT 058456 Medieval parts gone. Laird's aisle added in 1656 by Robert Baillie with fine south end window now forms altar end of 18th century church.

See also the main gazetteer entries for: Ayr, Biggar, Bothwell, Bute, Carnwath, Castle Semple, Covington, Douglas, Ladykirk, Lanark, Maybole, Rutherglen and Straiton.

Other medieval churches still in use: Glasgow Cathedral and Paisley Abbey.

Other former medieval churches: Cathcart, Dalserf, Dunlop, Eastwood, Inchinner, Irvine, Kilbarchan, Kilburnie, Kilmarnock, Kilmaurs, Largs, Thankerton, W. Kilbride

OTHER CHURCHES: BORDERS

ABBOTRULE NT 611127 Narrow single chamber, with square-headed doorway and good 17th century belfry. Abandoned in 1777.

ANCRUM NT 621248 Only foundations now remain.

AYTON NT 928609 St Dionysius. Main body 12th or 13th century. Burial aisle c1700.

BEDRULE NT 599179 Tiny robed effigy and two fragments of hog-back tomb-stones

BELFORD NT 815213 Foundations of 12th century nave and chancel by river.

BROUGHTON NT 110368 East end of church of St Liolan. Vault & window of 1617.

BUNKLE NT 809597 Vaulted Norman apse with two windows and two aumbries lies close to later church. Moulded arch towards the former nave demolished c1820.

CRAILING NT 688242 Only west wall and north of north wall now survive.

CRANSHAWS NT 684617 East gable and other low walling.

DRUMELZIER NT 134343 Small lancet and piscina suggest ruin is partly medieval.

DUNS NT 786543 12th century nave demolished in 1790. Chancel removed 1874.

EDNAM NT 738371 Burial enclosure includes possible 12th century north window.

ELLEM NT 727603 Foundations and fragment of the south wall still remain.

ETTLETON NY 472863 Window head, finial, cross-slabs & cross-shaft in enclosure.

FOGO NT 773492 Lower walls medieval. Upper walls rebuilt and aisle added 1683.

HAWICK NT 502144 T-plan kirk of 1764 may contain old walling. Dedicated to St Mary in 1214 and probably first built in 1150s. Remodelled in 1882-3 after a fire.

HENDERLAND NT 231234 Foundations of a small medieval chapel.

HERMITAGE NY 493960 Lower parts of 13th or 14th century chapel with several buttresses and two doorways lies in fenced enclosure to west of the castle.

HOBKIRK NT 587109 12th century pillar piscina, capitals, etc lie in church of 1869.

HOWNAM NY 777192 Church was originally cruciform. Shortened in 1752, and most features renewed in 1844, but round-arched late medieval doorway survives.

KILBUCHO NT 066318 Gables and low walls of possibly 13th century church.

KIRK YETHOLM NT 826281 Cross-slab by tower. 12th century fragments at manse.

LAMBERTON NT 968574 Plain walls of 12th century nave and 13th century chancel.

LENNEL NT 858411 Ruin, abandoned in 1705. Possibly part of it was vaulted.

LILLESLEAF NT 539254 Font in later churrch. Possible remains in burial enclosure.

LINDEAN NT 483308 Rebuilt low walls. Traces of SW doorway. Abandoned in 1586. 17th century Ker memorial in possible tomb recess on north side.

LONGFORMACUS NT 694572 Mostly rebuilt 1730 & 1892. 13th century cross-slab.

MAXTON NT 610303 St Cuthbert. 12th century, but rebuilt in 17th century & 1812.

Apse at Bunkle

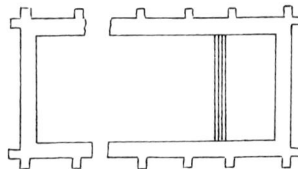
Plan of Hermitage Chapel

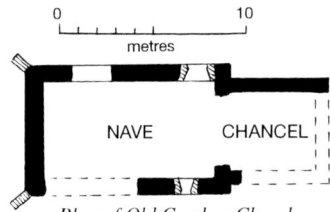
0   10
metres

NAVE   CHANCEL

Plan of Old Cambus Church

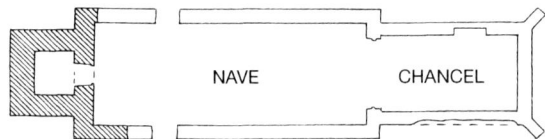
Low walls are shown unshaded

NAVE   CHANCEL

Plan of South Dean Church

*Note: Most places with little or no
standing medieval walling are not
included on this map, except those
with significant other features such
as old effigies, graveslabs or fonts.*

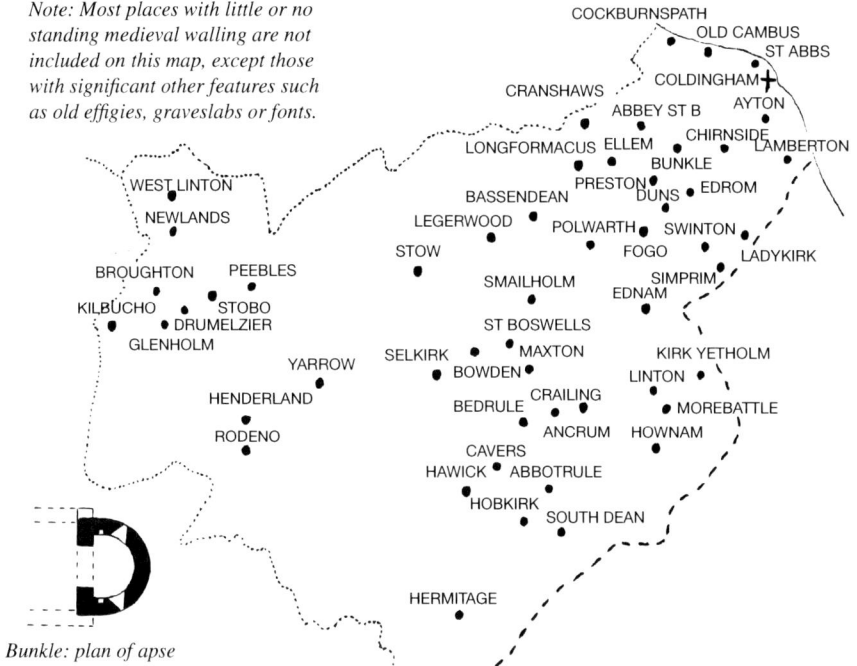

COCKBURNSPATH
OLD CAMBUS
ST ABBS
CRANSHAWS
COLDINGHAM
ABBEY ST B
AYTON
LONGFORMACUS ELLEM
CHIRNSIDE
LAMBERTON
BUNKLE
BASSENDEAN
PRESTON
DUNS
EDROM
WEST LINTON
LEGERWOOD
POLWARTH
SWINTON
NEWLANDS
STOW
FOGO
LADYKIRK
BROUGHTON
PEEBLES
SMAILHOLM
SIMPRIM
EDNAM
KILBUCHO
STOBO
DRUMELZIER
ST BOSWELLS
GLENHOLM
SELKIRK
MAXTON
KIRK YETHOLM
YARROW
BOWDEN
LINTON
HENDERLAND
BEDRULE
CRAILING
MOREBATTLE
RODENO
ANCRUM
HOWNAM
CAVERS
HAWICK
ABBOTRULE
SOUTH DEAN
HOBKIRK
HERMITAGE

Bunkle: plan of apse

MINTO NT 572203 Loose 12th century stones with chevrons, a nook-shaft base and
  capital and a cross-slab lie in overgrown enclosure just to south of the house.;
MOREBATTLE NT 773250 12th century church of St Laurence burned by English in
  1544. Rebuilt in 1757. Old work at SE corner. Foundations traced of possible tower.
OLD CAMBUS NT 804707 12th century nave has 14th century diagonal buttresses
  and two windows. No doorways remain. Only north wall remains of the chancel.
OXNAM NT 701190 Cross-slab by south wall of vestry of church mostly of 1738.
POLWARTH NT 750495 Dedicated 1242, rebuilt 1378 and 1703, when tower added.
RODENO NT 230189 Foundations of a medieval chapel at Chapelhope.
ST ABBS NT 917687 Traces of a medieval chapel to the south of the lighthouse.
SELKIRK NT 470283 Ruined T-plan kirk of 1748 on site used since the 12th century.
SIMPRIM NT 852454   Low walls of nave and chancel. Round arched east window.
SWINTON NT 839476 Effigy of a knight, in medieval style but perhaps actually later.
WEST LINTON NT 150156 Mostly rebuilt 1781. Arcaded reassembled font of c1200.
See also: Bassendean, Bowden, Cavers, Cockburnspath, Edrom, Ladykirk,
  Legerwood, Linton, Newlands, Peebles, Preston, South Dean, Stobo and Stow.
Parts of former monastic churches remain in use at Abbey St Bathans & Coldingham.
Sites of medieval church: Ashkirk NT 466220, Birgham NT 789390, Birselees NT
  577273, Castleton NY 508898, Eckford NT 706270, Eddleston NT 245471, Ettrick
  NT 260145, Foulden NT 931558, Glenholm NT 103330, Greenlaw NT 712461,
  Hume NT 700409, Kailzie NT 291382, Lyne NT 191405, Makerstoun NT 671317,
  Mertoun NT 625317, Mordington NT 947555, Nenthorn NT 687272, Nisbet NT
  674258, Roxburgh NT 701307, St Boswells NT 579315, Stichill NT 711382,
  Thirlstane NT 568478, Whitsome NT 862504, Yarrow NT 358278

OTHER CHURCHES: DUMFRIES & GALLOWAY

ANNAN NY 194665 19th century church on site of 12th century one destroyed by
    Lord Wharton in 1547. Edward I had used its tower as a munitions-store in 1299.

DALRY NX 618803 Burial aisle of Sir James Gordon d1547 by church of 1829.

DALTON NX 089747 Medieval footings under west, north & east walls of 1704 ruin.

DUMFRIES NX 975757 Church of St Michael of 1742-9 on site of medieval church.

DUMGREE NY 062967 Footings of small medieval chapel.

DUNROD NX 699466 Slight remains of small 12th century nave and chancel.

GIRTHON NX 606534 Windows of c1625, but ogee-arched piscina in SE corner.

GLENCAIRN NX 810903 End gables of church of c1200-40, each with two lancets,
    the east ones round-headed. 17th century round-headed doorway in west gable.

HODDOM NY 166727 Footings of late 13th or early 14th century buttressed nave
    and chancel near bridge. Traces of a north vestry. Old glass has been found here.

ISLE OF WHITHORN NX 480363 Small 13th century chapel of St Ninian by harbour
    has three original windows and a doorway. One later window also remains.

ISLES OF FLEET NX 574494 Larry's Isle is the site of a stone church of c800.
    Traces of an earlier wooden oratory were revealed by excavations.

KIRKBRIDE NT 855056 Small 16th century church of St Bridget has a north vestry
    with its own external doorway. Remains of south doorway and two small windows.

KIRKCONNELL NY 250754 Low walls reconstructed as part of 1926 excavation now
    deliniate former church of St Connell of c1300. Cross fragments in graveyard wall.

KIRKDALE NX 513540 Very ruined 13th century church with later SE doorway.

Isle of Whithorn chapel: plan

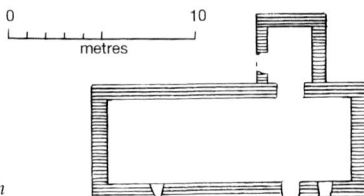

0   10
metres

Plan of Kirkbride Church

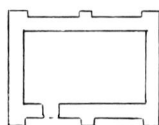

Lancet at Southwick

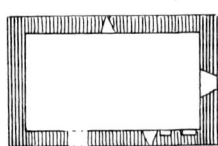

St Finian's: plan

■ 12th Century

▓ 13th Century

▤ 16th Century

▨ 17th Century

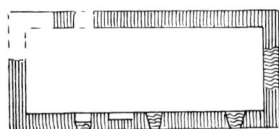

Plan of Kirkmadrine Church

St Cuthbert's Chapel, Moffat: window

Isle of Whithorn Chapel

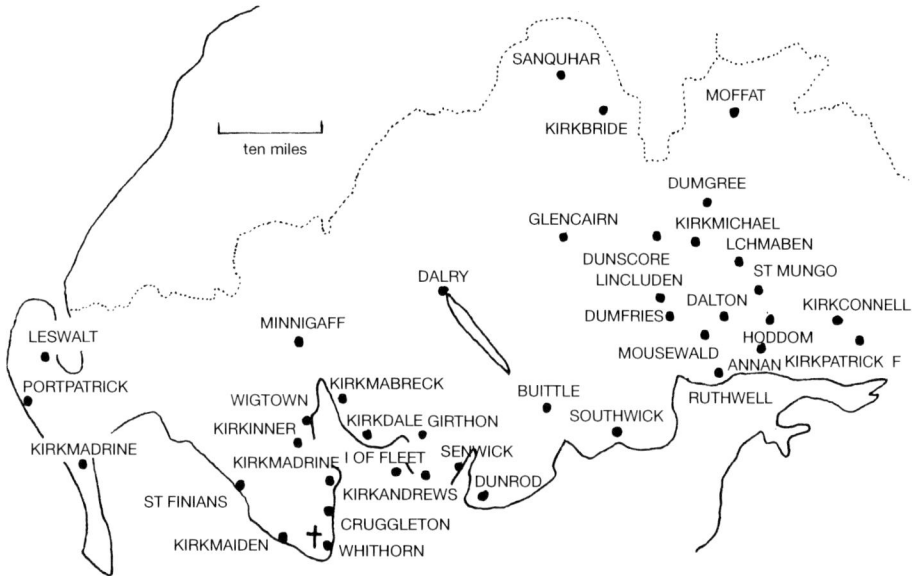

Map labels: SANQUHAR, MOFFAT, KIRKBRIDE, ten miles, DUMGREE, GLENCAIRN, KIRKMICHAEL, LCHMABEN, DUNSCORE, ST MUNGO, DALRY, LINCLUDEN, DALTON, KIRKCONNELL, MINNIGAFF, DUMFRIES, HODDOM, LESWALT, MOUSEWALD, ANNAN KIRKPATRICK F, PORTPATRICK, KIRKMABRECK, BUITTLE, RUTHWELL, WIGTOWN, KIRKDALE GIRTHON, SOUTHWICK, KIRKINNER, KIRKMADRINE, KIRKMADRINE I OF FLEET, SENWICK, KIRKMADRINE, DUNROD, ST FINIANS, KIRKANDREWS, CRUGGLETON, KIRKMAIDEN, WHITHORN

KIRKINNER NX 424515 10th century cross-slab now brought inside church of 1828.

KIRKMAIDEN NX 363400 Nave south doorway and blocked chancel arch could be late medieval. Chancel rebuilt to form the mausoleum of the Maxwells of Monreith.

KIRKMABRECK NX 493565 East gable and low walls of church abandoned 1637.

KIRKMADRINE NX 080484 12th century cross slab with interlace and leaft foot and early Christian grave slabs in porch of late 19th century mausoleum-chapel.

KIRKMADRINE N475482 13th century ruin. Windows all blocked up in 17th century.

KIRKMICHAEL NY 005884 Church rebuilt 1813. One half-buried graveslab of c1513.

KIRKPATRICK FLEMING NY 277701 Possible medieval walling in church of 1726.

LESWALT NX 015639 Ruined, ivyclad and much altered nave probably medieval.

MINNIGAFF NX 410666 Mostly 17th and 18th century but possible older window above east doorway and former tomb-recess in NE corner contains Celtic stones.

MOFFAT NT 070055 End gables of chapel of St Cuthbert of c1300 by farm. West window of three arched lights. Fragment of old parish church in the town centre.

MOUSEWOLD NY 065727 Worn effigy of knight of c1500 close to church of 1816.

PORTPATRICK NX 002543 Cruciform church 1629, and 16th century circular tower.

RUTHWELL NX 101683 Superb 8th century cross in church mostly of 1801 & 1906.

ST FINIANS NX 279489 Excavated footings of small early chapel with buttresses.

ST MUNGO NX 126756 East end of church of 1754. Stringcourse could be medieval.

SENWICK NX 655460 Rubble mound in graveyard of church abandoned in 1670.

SOUTHWICK NX 906569 St Mary's has two small lancets of c1200 in the east wall. Edward I of England donated 15 shillings for repairs to the church in 1300.

WIGTOWN NX 436555 Ivy-clad east and south walls of church of St Machutus. Aisle with tomb recess projects south. Another laird's aisle or vestry at the NE corner.

See also gazetteer entries for churches at: Buittle, Cruggleton and Lincluden.

Graveyards mark the sites of former churches of Dunscore (NX 904850), Kirkandrews (NX 601481) Kirkcudbright (NX 690512), Lochmaben (NY 082824). Other medieval churches probably at: Closeburn, Crossmichael, Garvald, Terregles & Torthorwald.

OTHER CHURCHES: FIFE

ABERCROMBIE NO 523034 Ruin near Balcaskie House probably late medieval. One east lancet. Bellcote and north doorway made of old tombstones c1600.

AUCHTERDERRAN NT 214960 North aisle 17th century. Main block rebuilt 1789.

AYTON NO 299184 No features of interest now survive in the ruin.

CERES NO 400118 Good 15th century effigy of knight in church of 1805-6.

EARLSFERRY NT 481994 Just one gable remains of a small chapel on a headland.

FORGAN NO 446259 Church of St Fillan c1500 with openings with chamfered edges. Transeptal north aisle with an arch with moulded imposts added c1600.

KINGLASSIE NT 228986 Medieval nave remodelled 1773-4. After the Reformation the chancel became a burial aisle and a transeptal north aisle was added.

MONIMAIL NO 299142 Round-arched tomb recess and sacaement house with two shields in low walls of chancel are probably 15th century. 17th century aisle intact.

MOONZIE NO 339177 Probable medieval masonry. Features of c1625 and 1821.

NEWBURN NO 453036 Small nave and chancel with piscina both probably 13th century. South doorway c1500. Transept, bellcote and blocked windows all later.

NORTH QUEENSFERRY NT 131804 West gable and fragment of north wall with round-arched doorway of chapel of St James rebuilt c1480 but existing by 1320s.

WEMYSS NT 340968 Mostly of 1528, when rebuilt. Chancel with original two-light window later used as Wemyss family burial aisle. Transepts of 1659. Secularised.

See also main gazetteer entries for: Abdie, Aberdour, Anstruther Wester, Burntisland, Carnock, Crail, Creich, Cupar, Dalgety, Dysart, Inverkeithing, Kilconquhar, Kinghorne, Kirkaldy, Leuchars, Markinch, St Andrews and St Monans.

Parts of former monastic churches at Dunfermline and Pittenweem remain in use.

The east parts of an abbey church at Culross became a parish church after 1560.

There may have once been medieval churches at Auchtermuchty and Falkland.

Interior of Abdie Church

Dalgety Church

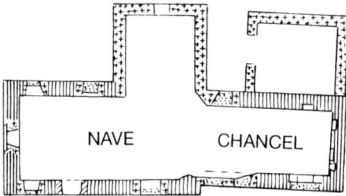

Plan of Newburn Church

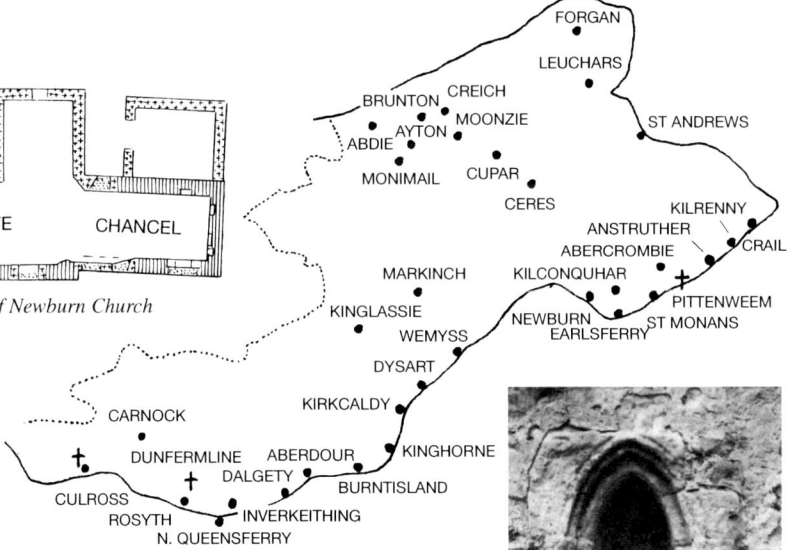

Map of Fife with locations:

FORGAN
LEUCHARS
CREICH
BRUNTON
MOONZIE
AYTON
ABDIE
ST ANDREWS
MONIMAIL
CUPAR
CERES
KILRENNY
ANSTRUTHER
ABERCROMBIE
CRAIL
MARKINCH
KILCONQUHAR
PITTENWEEM
KINGLASSIE
NEWBURN
ST MONANS
WEMYSS
EARLSFERRY
DYSART
KIRKCALDY
CARNOCK
DUNFERMLINE
ABERDOUR
KINGHORNE
DALGETY
CULROSS
BURNTISLAND
ROSYTH
INVERKEITHING
N. QUEENSFERRY

Chapel at Abercrombie

Aumbry at Carnock

Aumbry at Newburn

OTHER CHURCHES: HIGHLAND

ALLANGRANGE NH 625515 Eastern part of 13th century church with an aumbry and and triple lancets in east wall and a pair of lancets in the south wall.

AULDEAN NH 919556 Monuments lie within the ruined 16th century chancel with Y-tracery in east window to east of the church of 1754 remodelled in 1898.

AVOCH NH 874769 Reset sacrament house of c1500 within the church of 1870.

BOWER ND 244176 Wall bases must be medieval but no features earlier than 1718.

CADBOLL NH 874769 Buried footings of 13th century chapel of St Mary.

CILLE MUIRE NH 523773 Remote chapel with small windows. Doorway arch gone.

CONTIN NH 456557 Tomb recess and sacrament house date from just after church of St Maelrubha was burned by Macdonalds in 1480s. Rebuilt in 1730s and 1832.

COVINTH NH 512375 Fragments and footings of unusually wide medieval church.

CROMARTY NH 790674 Grave slab of c1500 in porch of late 16th century church with east vestry of 1700, north transept of 1739, and windows of 1756.

CROSSKIRK ND 025701 Tiny 12th century nave with original chancel arch and west doorway. No windows. South doorway is later. Chancel rebuilt as burial enclosure.

DINGWALL NH 550590 Easternmost of two burial enclosures north of church of 1799 is a relic of church of St Clement built in 1510. 15th century graveslab to south.

DRUMNADROCHIT NH 505303 East gable with medieval lancet surmounted by a shield with initials of Alexander Grant, minister 1624-45, by whom church rebuilt.

DUNLICHTY NH 660330 Medieval masonry, features all of 1757, 1829 and 1859.

DUNNET ND 220712 Church of St Anne with blocked NW doorway probably 16th century. Tower probably later. North transept of 1836. Windows more recent.

EDDERTON NH 710848 Church of 1743 may have old parts. Pictish slab by gateway.

GOLSPIE NC 831001 St Andrew. Rebuilt 1619 and replaced by T-plan kirk of 1736.

KILCHRIST NH 540492 13th century chapel retains piscina, aumbry, south doorway with drawbar slot and south window blocked at conversion to mausoleum c1870. The church was burned by the MacDonalds in 1603.

KILLEARNAN NH 576495 Blocked south doorway and SE window look 16th century Transepts 1745. Windows and new slate roof c1800. Small effigy inside west end.

KILMUIR NH 678502 Graham burial vault created in east end of church of c1500.

KILTARLITY NH 497439 Ruin of 1626 by river probably on site of medieval church. abandoned in 1764. Three-light east window with intersecting tracery may be later.

KILTEARN NH 616653 Medieval walling in main body widened in 1791 and traces of original east window. Transeptal aisle built by Munros of Foulis in 1743.

KINCARDINE NH 939155 Restored from ruin 1897. posswible lepers' squint. Party of Cummings burnt alive here in 16th century after their murder of the Grant chief.

KINCRAIG NH825048 Mackintosh mausoleum of 1780s lies inside 16th century chapel of St Drostan with round-arched windows.

KIRKHILL NH 549456 Lovatt Mausoleum of 1633 retains east wall of 13th century church with traces of large 14th century window sponsored by Lady Julia Ross.

KIRKMICHAEL NH 706658 Chancel has been rebuilt as Urquhart mausoleum. Fragmentary nave perhaps late medieval. Tomb recess remains on north side.

LATHERON ND 203334 Possible older lancet in burial aisle with monumen of 1640s.

NAIRN NH 885563 Fragment of church of 1658 on site of church of St Ninian.

NEWTON NH 846814 Footings only remain of a small medieval church.

NIGG NH 1626 Main body of 1626 on medieval footings. Pictish cross-slab inside.

NONAKILN NH 663712 St Ninian, Lintelled 17th century doorway inserted into arched older opening in west wall. Remainder of church reduced to foundations.

Plan of Crosskirk

ten miles

Allangrange: plan

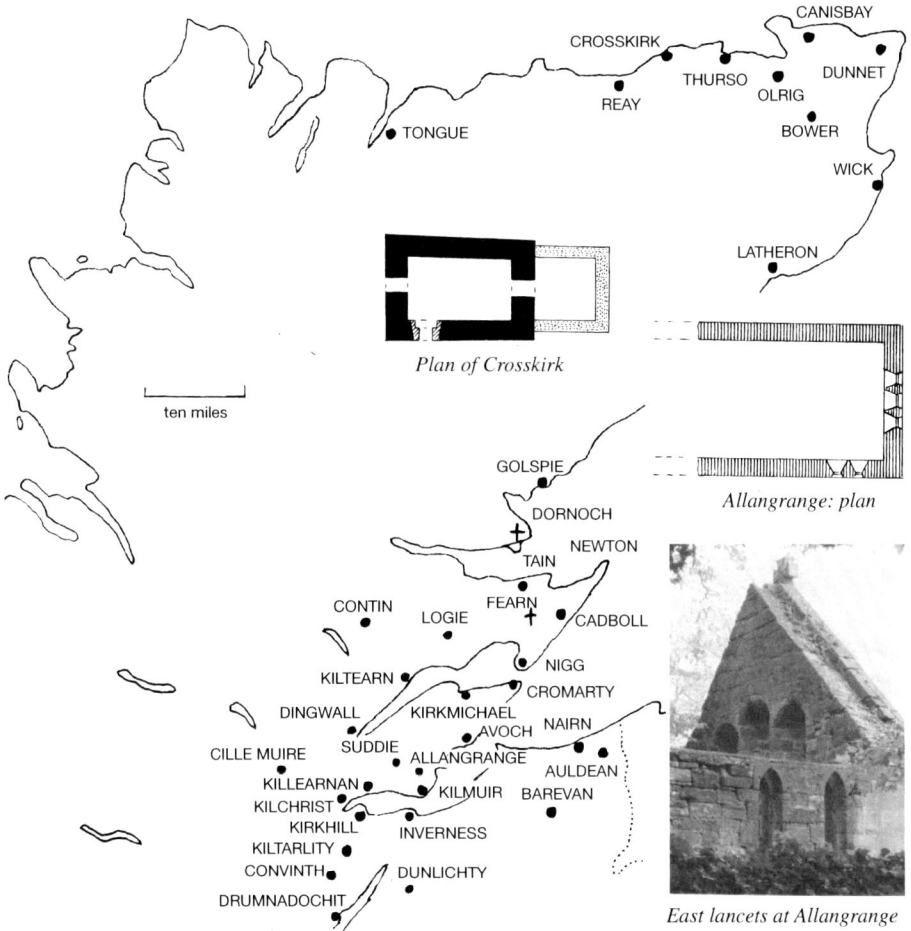

East lancets at Allangrange

OLRIG ND 186670 Blocked north doorway and one south window are 13th or 14th century. South windows and NW skewputt of 1633. SE skewputt dated 1743.

REAY NC 967649 Medieval slab and Mackay mausoleum of 1691 by 1738 church.

ROSEMARKIE NH 737577 Church now of 1818. Founded by St Boniface in the 7th century. Cathedral was here for a century before being moved to Fortrose in 1220s.

SUDDIE NH 666548 Just featureless east gable remains, probably late medieval.

TARBAT NH 915840 Footings and west gable may be medieval. Rebuilt in 1756.

TONGUE NC 591571 Main body partly medieval. South aisle of 1680, NE aisle 1728

WICK ND 363509 Only north aisle added c1590 to medieval church now remains.

See also gazetteer entries for: Barevan, Canisbay, Inverness, Tain and Thurso.

Still in use as parish churches are Dornoch Cathedral and Fearn Abbey Church.

Sites of other medieval churches: Abernethy NJ 005218, Alvie NH 864094, Ardersier NH 780567, Dalarossie NH 767242, Daviot NH 724395, Fodderty NH 512593, Killianan NH 572349, Kilmorack NH 494443, Kingussie NH 755010, Logie Easter NH 750761 or 753762, Petty NH 739499, Rosskeen NH 688694, St Martin's NH 640638, Urquhart NH 581585, Urray NH 506532

OTHER CHURCHES: ISLAY, JURA & COLONSAY

CILL NAOMH (KILNAVE) NR 285715 Late medieval chapel with west doorway with drawbar-slot, round-headed east and south windows and thick internal plastering. Supposedly burnt by the MacDonalds in 1598 when MacLeans took refuge here.

COLONSAY Minor remains of chapels of St Chattan and St Catherine, NR 362950, and 421998. Teampull A'Ghlinne, NR 374917 has north and south windows, a NW corner aumbry and a square-headed south doorway.

JURA NR 609822 Low walls of small Cill Chamuim Cille east of standing stones at Tarbert. Campbell Mausoleum of 1838 on site of former parish church at NR524687

KEILLS NR 414686 Late medieval chapel of St Columba has north & south windows

KILARROW NR 335625 Fragments remain in a boundary wall. Drawings of the 1770s show St Maelrubha's church with windows with 13th century type rere-arches.

KILCHIARAN NR 204601 Only east end with three aumbries and triangular-headed window still stands high of this thinly-walled and probably late medieval church.

KILCHOMAN NM 485640 Church now of 1825. Medieval cross & many cross-slabs

KILDALTON NR 458508 Two pointed east windows of c1200. Pairs of round-headed side windows, one with a grave-slab of knight in the blocking. North and south doorways (with drawbar-slots) out of line, suggesting a possible later lengthening.

KILNAUGHTON NR 344452 Grave-slab of knight in blocking of SE window. Two north windows, narrow eastern one, and two opposed north and south doorways.

NAVE ISLAND NR 291758 Small early 13th century chapel. Round-arched south windows. Later kelp-burning furnace set in NE corner.

ORSAY NR 164516 Late medieval church extended at east end to create a store. Original south doorway and north and south windows.

TEXA NR 390438 Small chapel of St Mary may be late 14th century. One window and a doorway with a drawbar-slot in south wall.

There are also slight remains of St Comgan's at Cill Chomlhan (NR 314411) and of St Columba's church at Nereabolls (NR 224548) The only pre-19th century church still in use is the round-naved building of 1767 at Bowmore (NR 311596)

Plan of Kildalton Church

East end of Kildalton Church

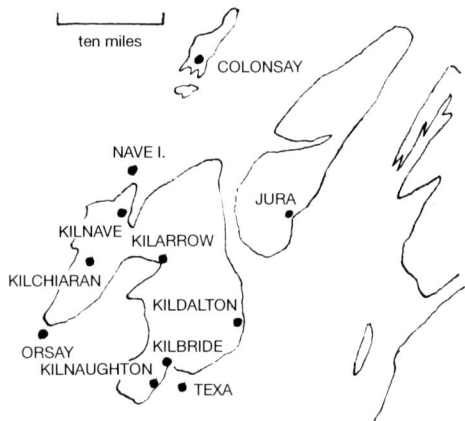

ten miles

COLONSAY
NAVE I.
JURA
KILNAVE
KILARROW
KILCHIARAN
KILDALTON
ORSAY
KILBRIDE
KILNAUGHTON
TEXA

Plan of Cill Naomi

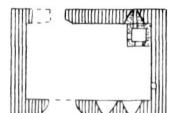

Nave Island: plan

CRAMOND NT 190769 Church of 1656 and later burial aisles lie on medieval site.

DUNBAR NT 682786 Church of 1818 on site of collegiate church founded in 1342 by Patrick, 9th Earl of Dunbar for a dean, archpriest and eight prebendary canons.

EAST CALDER NT 086678 Some walling may be as old as 12th century but north wall now missing and the rest divided up into several burial enclosures.

ECCLESMACHAN NT 058737 Lower parts of the main body and two south doorways with segmental hoodmoulds are of c1200. North transept added 1710.

GARVALD NT 591709 West and north walls are 12th century work with a lozenge pattern on a string-course. Sundial on south dated 1633. Transept added in 1677.

GOGAR NT 168725 16th century chancel beside later church of 1891, now disused. There are traces of the outline of the original east window.

KEITH MARISHALL NT 448646 Overgrown 13th century chancel with two east lancets hidden in trees near the house. Fragment of possibly older nave.

MORHAM NT 556726 Reused strip of 12th century carving on tiny church of 1724.

MOUNT LOTHIAN NT 275570 Lower parts remain of nave and small later chancel.

MUSSELBURGH NT 349729 Site of 16th century Loretto Chapel demolished c1590.

NEWBATTLE NT 331661 Seven sided font in church of 1727-9 possibly from abbey.

OLDHAMSTOCKS NT 738706 East wall clearly predates the Hepburn burial aisle of 1581 now converted into a chancel. North transept and other features are of 1701.

ORMISTON NT 411676 East end now burial enclosure. Alexander Cockburn, d1535 had a brass (now removed to National Museum in Edinburgh) over tomb recess.

SOUTRA NT 453584 Post-Reformation burial vault only. Hospital chapel now gone.

STENTON NT 623744 Saddleback-roofed tower set at SW corner of 16th century church with round-arched doorway.

TRANENT NT 403735 Northern part of wide church on footings of late 15th century. Outside is an incised slab to the priest Alexander Crawfurn, d1489.

See also main gazetteer entries for: Abercorn, Aberlady, Bathgate, Borthwick, Corstophine, Crichton, Dalkeith, Dalmeny, Duddingston, Dunglass, Edinburgh, Gullane, Haddington, Kirkliston, Lasswade, Linlithgow, Midcalder, North Berwick, Pencaitland, Prestonkirk, Ratho, Roslin, Restalrig, Seton, South Leith, Temple, Tyninghame, Uphall, Whitkirk and Yester.

Former monastic churches at South Queensferry and Torphichen also remain in use. Cranston, Currie, Innerwick, Inveresk & Livingston may have had medieval churches.

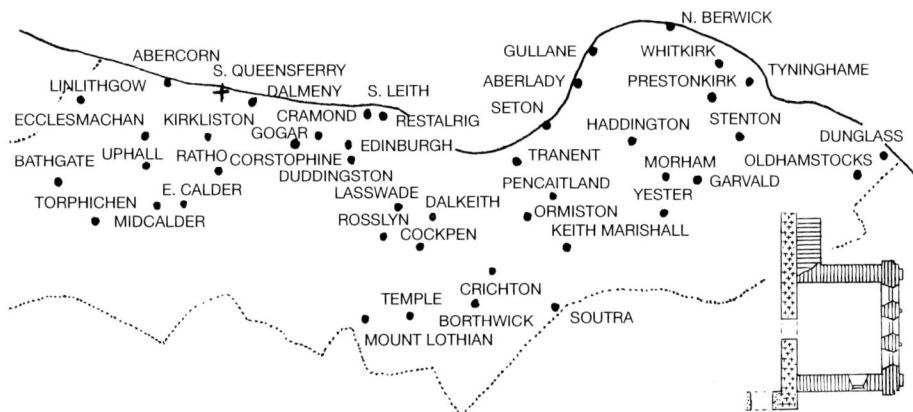

Prestonkirk: plan

OTHER CHURCHES: MULL, TIREE & MORVERN

ARISAIG NM 659869 Earlier chapel to west of St Maelrubha's church of c1560 built by John Moydartach, Captain of Clanranald, in which are 15th century grave-slabs.

GLEN AROS NM 545455 Foundations only of a 13th century chapel.

INCH KENNETH NM437354 13th century north doorway and four windows with rere-arches formed of thin slabs. The heavy east corner buttresses are later.

KILCHOAN NM 485640 Church of 1762 which had galleries incorporates walling of 12th or 13th century church of St Congan. On the Ardnamurchan peninsular.

LAGGAN M626236 Caibeal Mheamhair (Chapel of Remembrance) of c1200 given new roof and east wall in 1864 to form the mausoleum of Macleans of Lochbuie.

LOCHALINE NM 670451 Church of 1898 lies by burial enclosures on sites of later medieval transepts of which one arch set on semi-circular responds remains. 13th century original church of St Columba gone. Good collection of old graveslabs

PENNYGOWN NM 606432 13th century chapel with north doorway, round-headed west window and windows in north and south walls. No east window.

TIREE Chapel of St Kenneth (NL 943447) has a west doorways and a window in each bowed side-wall. Late 14th century chapel with round-arched west doorway and south windows and adjacent chapel at Kirkapoll (NM 042472) both dedicated to St Columba. Footings of St Patrick's chapel at Cean a Mhara (NL 937401), and fragments used as boundary markers alone remain at Soroby (NL 984416)

Only foundations remain at Kilvickeon (NM 412196), Killean (710284), Kilcolmkill at Dervaig (435517 - in use until 1754) and Kilfinichen (496284)

For churches on IONA see page 57.

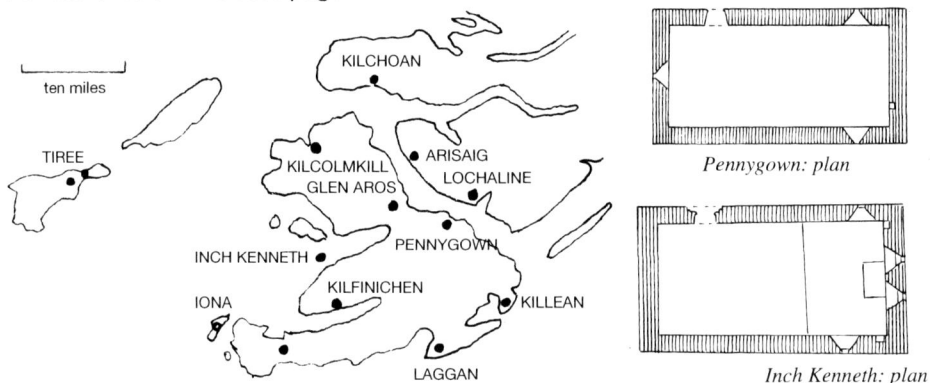

Pennygown: plan

Inch Kenneth: plan

The restored chapel at Laggan

BURWICK ND 440843 Church rebuilt 1788, but heraldic slabs remain of Sir Hugo
   Halcro, Rector of Ronaldsay, d1544 and James Kynnaird, d1624 and his wife.

DEERNESS NY 596088 On isolated rock above beach. 12th century chapel shown
   by excavation to have replaced 10th century timber-framed and stone clad chapel.

KIRKWALL HY 449109 Roll-moulded, round arched doorway of St Olaf's Church,
   dating from rebuilding of c1550 by Bishop Reid, hidden away in St Olaf's Wynd.

LINTON HY 530186 Just low walls remain of a nave and chancel.

PAPA WESTRAY HY 488527 Nave with slit window on north may be 12th century,
   like the hog-backed gravestone to the east. Other features and west end of c1700.
   Burial enclosure of the Traills of Holland on site of chancel. To the SW at 487508
   once lay the tiny church of St Tredwell.

PIEROWALL HY 440488 Ladykirk of 1674 uses footings and parts of south wall of a
   13th century church. 17th century Laird's loft with transomed east window has
   replaced the former chancel out of line with nave.

STENNESS HY 310125 Excavations in 1928 revealed footings of west tower said to
   have been circular to the west, although rising from a square base.

TUQUOY HY 455432 Low segmental-vaulted chancel and nave of Crosskirk both
   12th century. Round-headed doorway and window on south side. Western end with
   a second doorway is a later extension.

WYRE NY 444264 Tiny 12th centuy nave and chancel chapel near the castle.

See main gazetteer entries for: Birsay, Egilsay, Eynhallow and Orphir

Kirkwall Cathedral also remains in use.

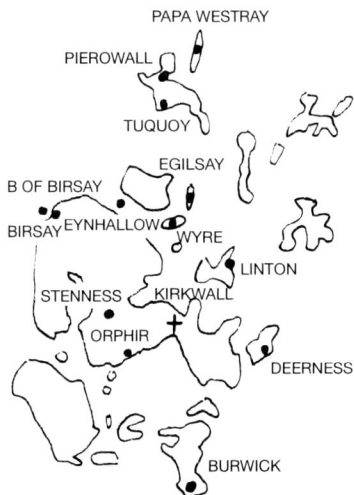

Crosskirk at Tuquoy: plan

Crosskirk at Tuquoy

Doorway of St Olaf's Church, Kirkwall

OTHER CHURCHES: PERTH & KINROSS

ABERUTHVEN NN 983152 Two small ogival-headed windows in east wall suggest a
    15th century date for the chancel of St Kattan's Church. Nave probably much older.

AUCHTERARDER NN 949141 Polygonal-headed piscina is the only feature of the
    quite sizeable but overgrown church of St Mackessog to the north of the town.

BENDOCHTY NO 218415 Now all of 1885, but with a worn and reset sacrament
    house, with initials of William Turnbull, d1526, and a stone commemorating a nun.

BLAIR ATHOLL NN867665 Mostly rebuilt c1570, when loft over vault added to south
    side. Windows mostly at gallery levels. Two medieval slabs on east side of vault.

CAMBUSMICHAEL NO 115326 Single chamber with tiny slit windows and a doorway
    Aumbry on north side. Ashlar blocks used in walls perhaps reset 12th century work.

CLEISH NS 095981 Medieval plain round font and cross-slab beside church of 1832.

COLLACE NO 197320 Arched doorway with dogtooth moulding is included in a
    fragment of medieval church within the Nairne mausoleum by the church of 1813.

DRON NO 296324 Fragments of late medieval chancel with chancel arch with semi-
    octagonal responds. No east window. Wider nave has gone.

ECCLESIAMAGIRDLE NO 107163 Small ruined chapel of possibly of c1500 hidden
    in dense foliage in estate. Restored and altered into a burial enclosure.

FOWLIS WESTER NN 928240 Long main body probably medieval. Several blocked
    16th and 17th century openings. North transept date uncertain. Victorian windows
    Two fine Pictish cross-slabs of c800, one from a chapel of St Bean at Buchanty.

GLENEAGLES NN 930090 Restored chapel with windows shuttered below glazing.
    East gable with intake and a reset finial from a 14th century buttress. Shield on SE
    skewputt refers to Margaret Erskine, who married Sir James Haldane in 1518.

KINFAUNS NO 166223 Refaced rib-vaulted 15th century south transept serves as
    burial aisle of Charteris and Grey families. Main body has a roll-moulded doorway.

KINKELL NN 937163 St Bean. Probably medieval but no features predate 1701.

LOGIE NS 815969 Just part of west gable remains with window sill dated 1598,
    and sundial of 1678. Originally 17m long and with a north aisle.

LOGIE ALMOND NO 010299 Featureless remains of small church of uncertain date.

LONGFORGAN NO 309300 Church of c1600, 1690, 1794, etc has varied collection
    of monuments, including incised slab of c1325 showing John de Galychtly and wife

MEIGLE NO 287447 Church of 1869 has octagonal font of c1500 with buttresses,
    ogee-headed panels with emblems of the Passion and Crucifixion. Most of the fine
    Pictish cross-slabs in museum came from churchyard.

Fowlis Wester Church

Doorway at Tullibardine

BLAIR ATHOLL
●

GRANDTULLY
WEEM ●
●
ten miles

AYLTH
●

BENDOCHTY
●

DRON
CAMBUSMICHAEL
DUNBLANE ●
✝
COLLACE
LOGIE
ROSSIE
METHVEN   PERTH
FOWLIS W.   ●   ●
RAIT
STROWAN ●   TIBBER
INNERPEFFRAY   ●   KINFAUNS
MUTHILL● KINKELL   MONCRIEFF
FORGANDENNY
TULLIBARDINE   ●
ABERUTHVEN ●   ABERNETHY
AUCHTERARDER   ●   ECCLESIAMAGIRDLE
●   DUNNING
GLENEAGLES
KINROSS
CLEISH

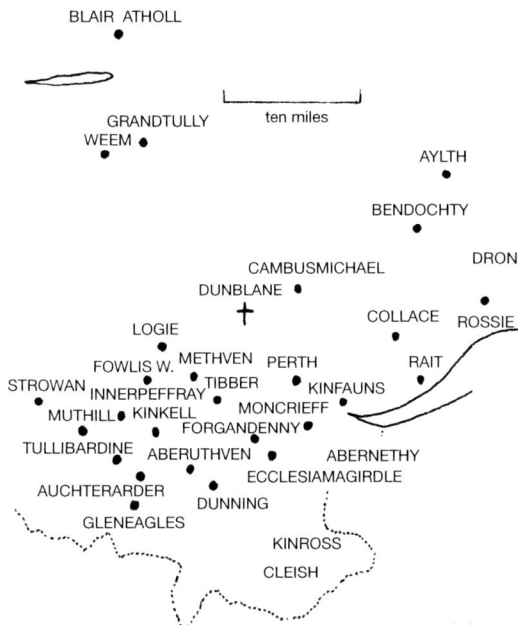

Pictish cross-slab at Fowlis Wester

Chapel at Gleneagles

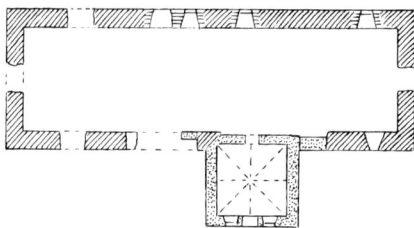

Plan of Kinfauns Church

MONCRIEFF NO 138193 Transepts and apse alater dded to a small nave with NE
aumbry and a tiny chapel on the north side.

RAIT NO 228269 Overgrown east and north walls remain, but without any features.

ROSSIE NO 291309 Angle-buttressed 13th century oblong altered as a mausoleum.
Contains fine Pictish cross-slab and an incised slab of c1260 of knight and wife.

STROWAN NN 821210 Eastern half remains of church of c1600, abandoned c1805.
On north side is a grave-slab of John Murray of Strowan, d1541.

TIBBERMORE NO052234 Features and east end 1789 but walling remains of church
of c1500 built by George Brown, Bishop of Dunkeld. Reset datestone of 1632.

WAST TOWN NO 240275 16th century nave with blocked arch at east end towards
a former chancel or burial aisle.

See also the main gazetteer entries for Abernethy, Alyth, Dunning, Forgandenny,
Grandtully, Innerpeffray, Methven, Muthil, Perth and Tullibardine

Dunkeld Cathedral remains partly in use. Kinross had a medieval church by L. Leven.

The churches at Dull, St Fillans and Weem may have medieval walling or foundations.

OTHER CHURCHES: SHETLAND

BRESSAY HU 522223 Low drystone walls of church of St Mary at Cullingsburgh. It has a north transept, and there may once have been a south transept.

CROSSKIRK HU 213780 Lowest courses remain of a medieval single chamber with a west doorway at Esha Ness.

CROSSKIRK HP 650121 Footings at Clibberswick of a drystone nave to which has been added a shallow chancel. Footings remain of of other chapels on Unst at Haroldswick HP 636128, and Norwick HP 652141.

FAIR ISLE Slight remains of small chapels at HU 631909 and 629911

FRAMGORD HP 619029 Drystone walls of 11th or 12th century chapel with west doorway. Nearby lie several contemporary cross-slabs.

GLETNA HP 593020 Footings only of church of uncertain date.

HOLM OF SHAW HU 600674 Footings of a chapel on Whalsay.

LUNDAWICK HP 566042 12th century chapel with original west doorway and small windows on north and south. East end with just a south window is later.

LUNNA HU 486691 Buttresses at east side of harled church of 1753 form Hunter burial enclosures. One has a squint which may be a relic of a medieval chapel.

NORTH YELL HP532050 Excavations have revealed lower parts of the nave of the Kirk of Ness with a blocked west dooway and a later SW doorway, plus a chancel with windows and aumbries on either side but the east wall mostly destroyed.

ST NINIANS HU 368208 Excavations in 1950s revealed footings of small 12th century nave to which was added an apsidal chancel. Here was found a Pictish hoard of silver objects hidden from Vikings c800, now in an Edinburgh museum.

SANDWICK HP 618028 Segmental late medieval chancel arch and stubs of nave walls of St Mary's church in graveyard by shore. Drystone walls mark out a chancel.

UYEA HU 608985 Tiny windowless nave with blocked west doorway facing into later vestry with north doorway. Arch to vanished chancel is no wider than a doorway.

Plan of Lundawick Church

Lundawick Church

Flamgord Chapel

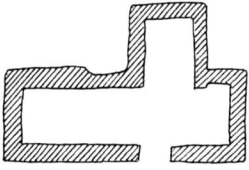

Plan of Cullingsburgh Church

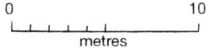

0   10
metres

Plan of North Yell Church

Plan of St Ninian's Church

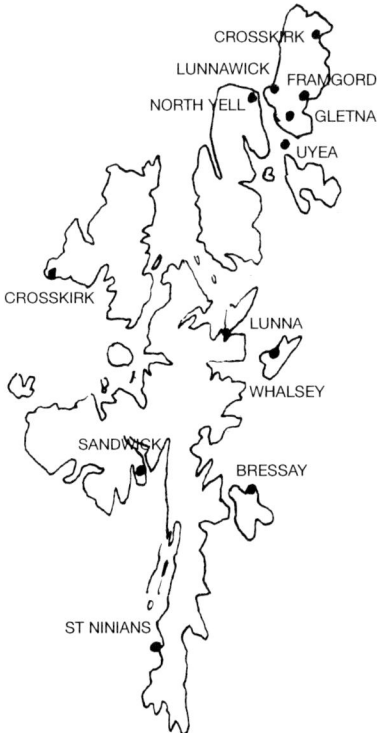

Cullingsburgh Church, Bressay

CROSSKIRK
LUNNAWICK
NORTH YELL   FRAMGORD
GLETNA
UYEA
CROSSKIRK
LUNNA
WHALSEY
SANDWICK
BRESSAY
ST NINIANS

St Ninian's Church

Chancel arch at Sandwick

OTHER CHURCHES: SKYE & LOCHABER

CILLE CHOIRILL NN 307813 Chapel of St Cyril high above Roy Bridge restored as
   a Catholic chapel in 1933. Round-arched SE window may be 13th century.
CILLE CHRIOSD NG 617207 16th century chapel with south windows rebated for
   internal shutters. 18th century MacKinnon burial enclosure adjoins.
CILLE DHONNAIG NM 565538 Traces of church replaced 1780 by one at Fernish.
DUIRINISH NG 255478 Macleod burial place. St Mary's Church is only of 1689, etc.
EIGG NM 488853 Medieval cross-shaft with scroll vine patters and pairs of animals
   near church built c1570 by John Moydartach with arched tomb recess of 1641.
EILEAN MUNDE NN 083591 Traces of late medieval doorway and two windows on
   south side. North wall now quite low and the rest much defaced.
EYNORT NG 376260 Late medieval chapel beside 17th century church contains
   18th century Macleod monuments. Cross-shaft with bishop and rosettes nearby.
GLENDALE NG 177498 Graveslab of harper remains, but chapel itself now gone.
KEILL NM 971538 Possibly of c1200. Two aumbries in SE corner, south window, a
   wider north window, west window set high up, and gap of former NW doorway.
KILMALLIE NN 092770 Burial enclosure of Camerons of Fassifern to west of the
   church of 1781 may have once been a north transept of the 16th century church.
KILMALUAG NG 436749 West gable and footings of chapel of St Martin.
KILMUIR NG 389706 Graveslab depicts knight in armour. Chapel itself now gone.
KINLOCHLAGGAN NN 536897 Most of walling now a drystone replacement, but a
   tomb recess remains on south side of this chapel of St Kenneth.
KINTAIL NG 946212 South doorway is 16th century or of 1649. Bombarded in 1719
   by frigate during attack on Eilean Donan Castle. Repaired 1739. MacRae tombs.
LOCH PORTREE NG 484423 Footings of chapel of St Columba on islet.
RAASAY NG 552370 Church of St Moluag with round-headed east window and
   pointed west one may be 13th century. West gable had three small lancets. Later
   tomb recess in SE corner. A west gallery was inserted after the Reformation.
SKEABOST NG419485 Footings of 16th century church on island. Adjacent late
   medieval chapel of St Columba with slab depicting warrior. Two more slabs nearby
TORVAIG NG 497444 Minor remains of chapel above the shore NE of Portree.
TRUMPAN NG 225612 Mere slit for east window. Two walls are reduced to footings.
   NE window and a slightly pointed NW doorway. Probably late medieval.

Plan of Trumpan Church

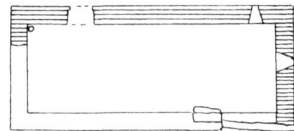

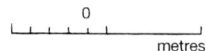

0   10

metres

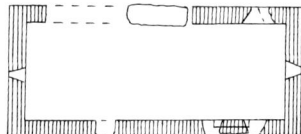

Trumpan Church   *St Moluag's Church, Raasay, plan*

KILMALUAG

TRUMPAN

GLENDALE
DUIRINISH SKEABOST
TORVAIG
PORTEE
RAASAY

EYNORT
CILL CHRIOSD
KINTAIL

EIGG
CILLE DHONNAIG

KINLOCHLAGGAN

KILMALLIE
CILLE CHOIROLL

ten miles

EILEAN MUNDE
KEIL

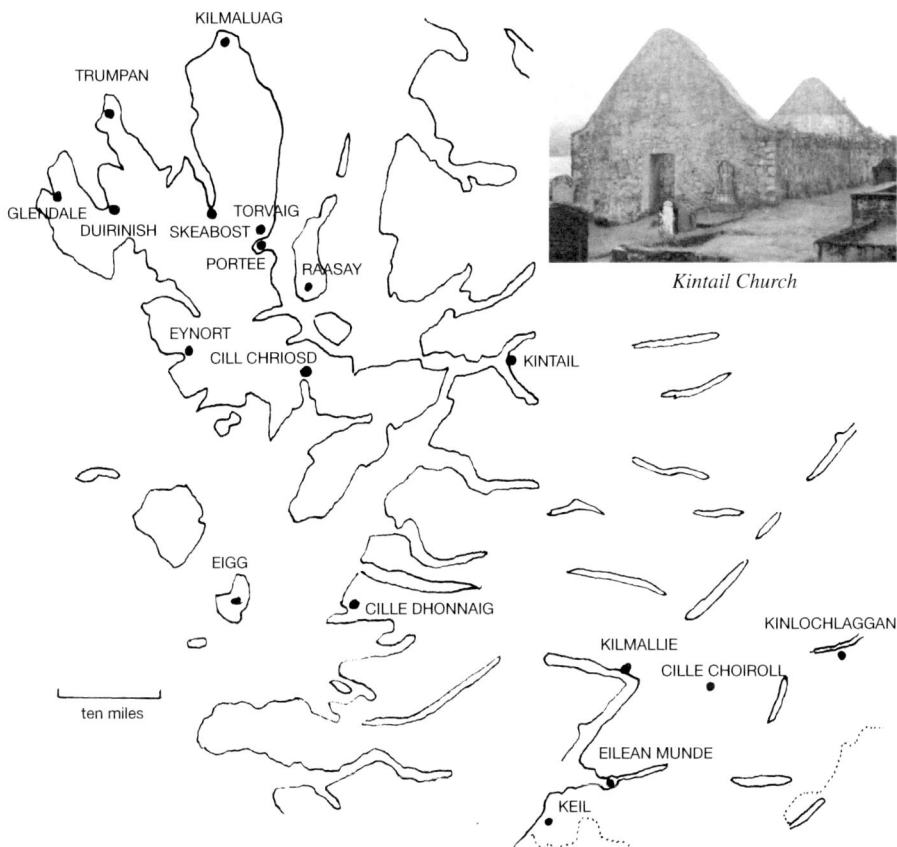

Kintail Church

Effigy at Skeabost

Raasay Church

OTHER CHURCHES: STIRLING & FALKIRK

ALLOA NS 884926 Church of Old St Mungo in Kirkgate mostly demolished in 1817, leaving only west tower and adjoining parts of nave, both essentially of 1681-3.

BALQUIDDER NN 536210 Slight traces of medieval church lie beside graves of Rob Roy MacGregor, d1734 and family. Ruined church to the west is of 1613 and later.

BLACKNESS NT 055799 Chapel of St Ninian destroyed by use as gun-emplacement for Cromwellian siege of castle in 1650. Low walls of probably 13th century nave and chancel and of a later medieval south transept stand on hill south of castle.

CAMPSIE NS 610797 West wall with 17th century doorway and stepped gable plus part of north wall remains of church of St Machen said to have been 23m long.

FINTRY NS 626862 Church of 1823 has a bell of 1626 upon its tower. It replaced a building of 1626 which was the successor of a 13th century building.

INCHCAILLEACH NS 410906 Foundations of late 12th or early 13th century nave and chancel church of St Kentigern on island in Loch Lomond. Abandoned in 1621. Excavated 1903. A MacGregor tomb of 1693 lies in the rectangular graveyard.

KILBRYDE NN756027 Mausoleum of 1864 appears to have older work in north wall.

KILMADOCK NO 7322021 East wall with later doorway below medieval lancet by two burial enclosures. Church of St Bean repaired c1680 but unroofed in 18th cent.

KIRKINTILLOCK NS 655740 Cruciform church of 1644 replaced medieval church. A chapel of St Mary stood in a graveyard in Old Aisle Road to SE at NS 666733.

ST BRIDE NN 585099 Only foundations remain of a small medieval chapel-of-ease. East end has one step up. Fragment of Early Christian cross lies in the graveyard.

ST NINIANS NS 796916 16th century chancel with aumbry and piscina forms Murray burial enclosure. 15th century nave destroyed in 1746 by explosion of gunpowder stored within it by Jacobites, but dome-roofed west tower of 1734 still remains.

TILLICOULTRY NS 924976 Graveyard with 12th century hogback stone and also 16th century and later memorials marks the site of a medieval chapel.

See main gazetteer entries for churches at : Airth, Falkirk, Kinneil, Stirling & Tullibdy.

Dunblane Cathedral also still remains in use for services.

Blair Drummond, Clackmannan and Kirkintilloch may have had medieval churches.

The last traces of St Bride's Chapel

BALQUIDDER
ST BRIDE'S KILBRYDE
DUNBLANE
KILMADOCK
TULLICOULTRY
INCHCAILLEACH FINTRY STIRLING TULLIBODY
ALLOA
AIRTH
CAMPSIE ST NINIANS
KINNEIL
KIRKINTILLOCH FALKIRK
BLACKNESS

ten miles

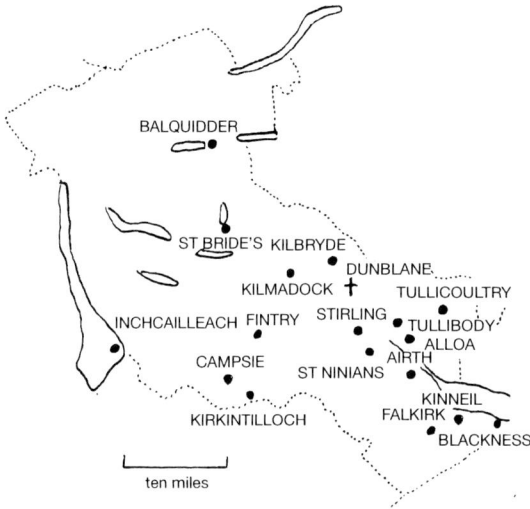

Last remains of Kilmaddock church

Aisle vaulting at Stirling

The chancel at Stirling

OTHER CHURCHES: WESTERN ISLES

BENEBECULA NF 782549 Church of St Malcolm has rectangular windows and west
doorway in nave, and a narrower, thinner walled chancel added in 16th century.
Nunton chapel to SE at NF 766537 has a niche for a statue over the west doorway.

BRAGAR NB 288489 Slit windows remain in the nave and chancel of church of St
John. Footings of later L-plan building to south of the chancel.

ENSAY NF 981866 Small late medieval chapel with south doorway and narrow
loops in each wall, one on north being blocked up. Step for altar at the east end.

GALSTON NB 433594 Half-buried low walls of 12th or 13th century chapel of Holy
Blood (Teampull Nan Cro Naomb). SW doorway with drawbar slots. Small south
window, larger north window. Little remains of the end walls.

GRESS NB 490416 Chapel dated 1681 with initials I.B. and M.K. contains medieval
walling and is said to have been dedicated to St Olaf.

GRIMSAY NF 883547 West gable and footing of other walls of chapel of St Michael.

NORTH RONA HW 809323 Chapel on remote island far to NE of Butt of Lewis. Tiny
original chapel with west doorway and originally roofed with slabs of gneiss later
became chancel of a wider nave with a south wall rebuilt in 1938 partly 1.5m thick.

NORTHTON NF 970714 Small chapel with slit window in each wall, the western
set higher up. Steps at either end and seating for an altar. Beside this is a corbel
for a statue and a pair of aumbries.

NORTH UIST NF 816603 Church of Holy Trinity said to have been built c1200 by
Bethoc, daughter of Somerled. Largest of the Western Isles churches until Rodel
was built in 1520s. Walls pierced by square holes. Jamb of one NE window also
remains near where a passage leads to a late medieval sacristy or chapel.

PABBAY NF 890870 Side walls and west gable with rectangular doorway and slit
window survive of Teampull Mhoire. Little remains of Teampull Beag to the west.

SOUTH UIST NF 756365 Teampull Mor, parish church of Howmore, has two east
lancets with segmental heads and round rere-arches. This end and a later building
to SE alone stand high. Similar east window in the adjacent Caibeal Dhiamaid.

SWAINBOST NB 508638 East window with slit window and footings of north and
south walls remain of medieval church of St Peter remodelled and enlarged c1790.

See also main gazetteer entries for: Barra, Europie, Eye and Rodel.

St Barr's Church, Barra

Holy Trinity Church, North Uist

Rodel: window

ten miles

EUROPIE
GALSTON
SWAINBOST
BRAGAR
GRESS

LEWIS

EYE

HARRIS

PABBAY
NORTHTON
RODEL

NORTH UIST

BENBECULA
GRIMSAY

SOUTH
UIST

BARRA

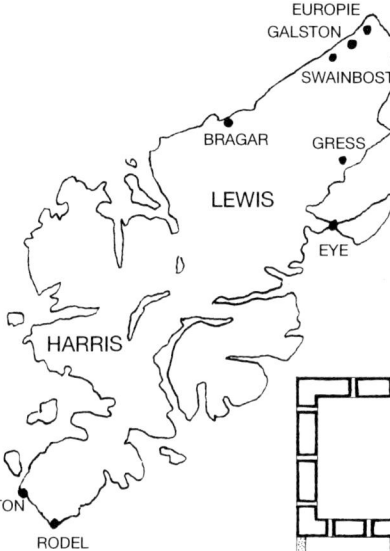

Cille Barra; plan of main church

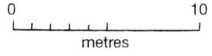

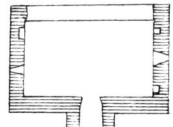

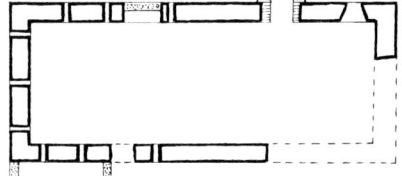

0   10
metres

Holy Trinity Church, North Uist: plan

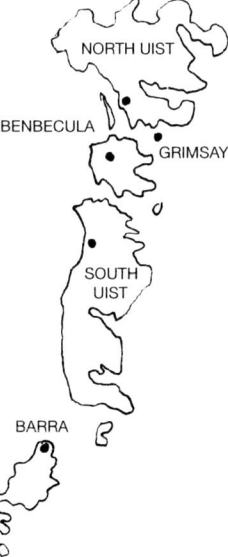

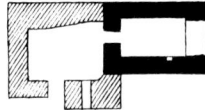

■	12th Cent
□	c1200
⦀	13th Cent
▨	15th Cent
▤	16th Cent

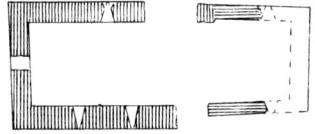

North Rona: plan

St Malcolm's Church, Benbecula

Cille Barra, showing the church and the two chapels

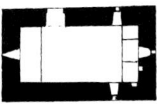

Northton Chapel: plan

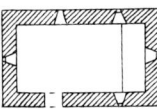

Ensay Chapel: plan

St John's Church, Bragar

INDEX OF CHURCHES

Entries with an asterisk are Cathedrals or Abbey Churches not fully described in this book
Entries in italics are places with no medieval walling, furnishings or monuments left on site.

GLOSSARY OF TERMS

Aisle	-	A passage beside part of a church.
Apse	-	A semi-circular chapel or a similarly shaped east end of a church.
Ashlar	-	Masonry of large blocks cut to even faces and square edges.
Aumbry	-	A recess for storing books or vessels.
Bays	-	Divisions of an elevation defined by regular vertical features.
Caphouse	-	Small wall-head chamber, usually a top of a spiral staircase.
Cartouche	-	A classical style memorial tablet with an ornate frame.
Chancel	-	The eastern member of a church reserved for priests and choristers.
Chevrons	-	Vs usually arranged in a continuous sequence to form a zigzag.
Choir	-	Part of a monastic church containing stalls for monks, nuns or friars.
Clerestory	-	An upper storey pierced by windows lighting the floor below.
Coffering	-	Sunken panels decorating the underside of an arch or ceiling.
Corbel	-	A projecting or overhanging stone bracket.
Crow Steps	-	Squared stones forming steps on a gable. The lowest is a skewputt.
Cruciform Church	-	Cross-shaped church with transepts forming the arms of the cross.
Cusps	-	Projecting points between the foils of a foiled Gothic arch.
Dado	-	Lower part of a wall, or its decorative treatment.
Dog-tooth	-	Four cornered stars placed diagonally and raised pyramidally.
Fleuron	-	Decorative carved shape like a flower or leaf.
Harling	-	A form of roughcasting, usually of aggregate and lime.
Hood-moulding	-	A narrow band of stone projecting out over a window or doorway.
Jamb	-	The side of a window, doorway or open opening.
Lancet	-	A long and comparatively narrow window, usually pointed headed.
Light	-	A compartment of a window.
Loop Tracery	-	Tracery dividing a series of simple loops or goblet shapes.
Mullion	-	A vertical member dividing the lights of a window.
Nave	-	The part of a church in which the lay congregation stood or sat.
Ogival Arch	-	Topped by a curve which is partly convex and partly concave.
Pilaster	-	Flat buttress or pier attached to a wall. Usual in the 12th century.
Piscina	-	A stone basin used for rinsing out holy vessels after a mass.
Quoin	-	A cut stone used to form part of a corner.
Pulpitum	-	A stone screen dividing a choir of a major church from the nave.
Rere-arch	-	An arch on the inside face of a window embrasure or doorway.
Respond	-	Half pier bonded into a wall and carrying one end of an arch.
Reticulation	-	Window tracery with a net-like appearance.
Rood Screen	-	A screen with a crucifix mounted on it between a nave and chancel.
Sacrament House	-	Ornate safe cupboard for the reserved sacrament.
Sacristy	-	A part of a church were vestments and sacred vessels were kept.
Saddleback Roof	-	A plain gabled roof set upon a tower.
Sedilia	-	Seats for clergy (usually three) in south wall of a chancel or choir.
Spandrel	-	The surface between two arches or between an arch and a corner.
Teind	-	The tenth part of revenues of an estate or farm, due to the church.
Tierceron	-	Intersecting ribwork in the upper part of a later Gothic window.
Tracery	-	Extra decorative vaulting ribs springing from the corners of a bay.
Transept	-	A cross-arm projecting at right-angles from main body of a church.
Transom	-	A horizontal member dividing upper and lower lights in a window.
Vesica Window	-	A pointed oval or eye-shaped opening.
Voussoir	-	Small wedge shaped stone used as part of an arch.